THE FINEST GARDENS
OF THE SOUTH WEST

After studying forestry and horticulture in the early 1980s, Tony Russell's career with plants has taken him from Snowdonia to the New Forest in Hampshire, then to Westonbirt Arboretum in Gloucestershire – where he was Head Forester for thirteen years – and recently back to Snowdonia. Tony is a familiar face and voice on TV and radio, presenting a number of TV series such as *Garden Trail*, *Roots & Shoots*, *Britain's Great Trees*, *Saving Lullingstone Castle* and featuring on BBC Radio 4 in series such as *Invasive Plants* and on *Gardeners' Question Time*. He is also a regular contributor to the gardening pages of national newspapers such as *The Telegraph* and national magazines such as *BBC Gardeners' World Magazine*.

The Finest Gardens of the South West is Tony's fifteenth book and follows on from such best-selling titles as *The World Encyclopaedia of Trees*, *Cornwall's Great Gardens*, *Westonbirt: A Celebration of the Seasons*, *Tree Spotting for Children* and *The Cotswolds' Finest Gardens*. He is also editor of the annual publication *Great Gardens to Visit* and the magazine *Discover Britain's Gardens*.

In addition to his broadcasting and writing, Tony runs a thriving consultancy that provides advice and guidance on gardens to private owners, charitable trusts and UK-wide organisations such as the National Trust. Tony is an avid botanical traveller and regularly leads tours for plant and garden enthusiasts to locations across the world, including the Himalayas, Amazonia, China, Japan, New Zealand and India.

For more information visit:
www.gardenstovisit.net
www.amberley-books.com

THE FINEST GARDENS
OF THE SOUTH WEST

TONY RUSSELL

AMBERLEY

Dunster Castle – Bananas on the Castle Terrace

This edition first published 2015

Amberley Publishing
The Hill, Stroud,
Gloucestershire, GL5 4EP
www.amberley-books.com

Principal photographer Tony Russell; text and
photographic copyright © Tony Russell, 2015

The right of Tony Russell to be identified as the
Author of this work has been asserted in accordance
with the Copyrights, Designs and Patents Act 1988.

ISBN 978 1 4456 4124 9 (print)
ISBN 978 1 4456 4136 2 (ebook)

British Library Cataloguing in Publication Data.
A catalogue record for this book is available from the
British Library.

Printed in the UK.

Photo page 1 – Hestercombe

INTRODUCTION

The West Country of England is probably one of the best regions in the UK for growing plants that are native to other parts of the world, in particular tender and sub-tropical plants. This is mainly due to the effects of the Gulf Stream and North Atlantic Drift, which regularly bathe the western fringes of Britain with relatively warm, moist air. This does not mean that summers are necessarily hotter here but rather that winters are milder. Consequently, tender plants are able to survive more easily in the West Country than in other regions of Britain. As a result, over the past two and a half centuries, an astonishing collection of plants and indeed gardens have been established here.

While in recent years this is something that has become recognised in relation to Cornwall, it is something that perhaps has not yet been fully appreciated for the other West Country counties, namely Devon, Dorset and Somerset. This book attempts to rectify this situation and portray to the world just what an amazing collection of plants and gardens there are in South West England.

Through my work, I have, over a period spanning more than twenty-five years, been fortunate enough to spend many happy hours exploring the gardens in this region and it never ceases to amaze me just how exciting and diverse the collection is. From the crazy mix of sub-tropical and southern hemisphere plants established in the Abbey Gardens on Tresco and at Abbotsbury in Dorset, to the remarkable architectural, cosmopolitan, twentieth-century gardens at Compton Acres near Bournemouth, with their Asian and Italian influences, these are gardens that constantly surprise and push the horticultural boundaries. The highlights are too many to mention here, but memories of magnolias flowering at Caerhays Castle, Jekyll and Lutyens' rose-draped Edwardian creation at Hestercombe, high summer among the butterfly-rich borders of Thomas Hardy's cottage garden in Higher Bockhampton and the fiery autumn leaves of Castle Hill and Marwood Hill will undoubtedly stay with me forever.

My difficulty has not been in finding fifty gardens to include in this book, rather deciding which ones to leave out; I could have included at least another fifty. In the end the final selection is what I feel best portrays the diversity of this region. I leave it to you, the reader and garden visitor, to judge if that is the case.

Tony Russell
January 2015

✺ THE LIST OF GARDENS

❀ THE LIST OF GARDENS

FEATURED GARDENS

ABBOTSBURY SUBTROPICAL GARDENS
Buller's Way, Abbotsbury,
Weymouth, Dorset, DT3 4LA
Tel: 01305 871387
www.abbotsbury-tourism.co.uk/
gardens

ANTONY
Torpoint, Cornwall, PL11 2QA
Tel: 01752 812191
www.nationaltrust.org.uk/antony

ARLINGTON COURT
Arlington, Devon, EX31 4LP
Tel: 01271 850296
www.nationaltrust.org.uk/
arlington-court

ATHELHAMPTON HOUSE GARDENS
Athelhampton, DT2 7LG
Tel: 01305 848363
www.athelhampton.co.uk

BARRINGTON COURT
Barrington, Somerset, TA19 0NQ
Tel: 01460 242614
www.nationaltrust.org.uk/
barrington-court

BENNETTS WATER GARDENS
Putton Lane, Dorset, DT3 4AF
Tel: 01305 785150
www.bennettswatergardens.com

BURROW FARM GARDENS
Burrow Farm, Devon, EX13 7ET
Tel: 01404 831285
www.burrowfarmgardens.co.uk

CAERHAYS CASTLE GARDEN
Gorran, Saint Austell, PL26 6LY
Tel: 01872 501310
www.caerhays.co.uk

THE WALLED GARDENS OF CANNINGTON
Cannington, Somerset, TA5 2HA
Tel: 01278 655042
www.canningtonwalledgardens.
co.uk

CASTLE DROGO
Drewsteignton, Exeter, Devon,
EX6 6PB
Tel: 01647 433306
www.nationaltrust.org.uk/
castle-drogo

CASTLE HILL GARDENS
Filleigh, Barnstaple, Devon,
EX32 0RH
Tel: 01598 760336
www.castlehilldevon.co.uk

CHALICE WELL GARDENS
85-8 Chilkwell Street, Glastonbury,
Somerset, BA6 8DD
Tel: 01458 831154
www.chalicewell.org.uk

COMPTON ACRES
164 Canford Cliffs Road, Poole,
Dorset, BH13 7ES
Tel: 01202 707591
www.comptonacres.co.uk

COTEHELE
Saint Dominick, Saltash, PL12 6TA
Tel: 01579 351346
www.nationaltrust.org.uk/cotehele

COTHAY MANOR
Greenham, Nr. Wellington,
Somerset, TA21 0JR
Tel: 01823 672283
www.cothaymanor.co.uk

DUNSTER CASTLE AND GARDENS
Minehead, Dunster, Somerset,
TA24 6SL
Tel: 01643 823004
www.nationaltrust.org.uk/
dunster-castle

EAST LAMBROOK MANOR GARDENS
East Lambrook, South Petherton,
TA13 5HH
Tel: 01460 240328
www.eastlambrook.co.uk

THE EDEN PROJECT
Bodelva, Cornwall, PL24 2SG
Tel: 01726 811911
www.edenproject.com

FORDE ABBEY GARDENS
Forde Abbey, Chard, Dorset,
TA20 4LU
Tel: 01460 220231
www.fordeabbey.co.uk

GLENDURGAN
Glendurgan, Falmouth, Cornwall,
TR11 5JZ
Tel: 01326 252020
www.nationaltrust.org.uk/
glendurgan-garden

GREAT CHALFIELD MANOR
Melksham, Wiltshire, SN12 8NH
Tel: 01225 782239
www.nationaltrust.org.uk/
great-chalfield-manor

GREENCOMBE
Greencombe, Porlock, Minehead,
Somerset, TA24 8NU
Tel: 01643 862363
greencombe.wordpress.com

HARDY'S COTTAGE
Hardy's Cottage,
Higher Bockhampton, Dorchester,
Dorset, DT2 8QJ
Tel: 01305 262366
www.nationaltrust.org.uk/
hardys-cottage

HESTERCOMBE
Hestercombe Gardens, Taunton,
TA2 8LG
Tel: 01823 413923
www.hestercombe.com

KILLERTON
Broadclyst, Exeter, Devon,
EX5 3LE
Tel: 01392 881345
www.nationaltrust.org.uk/
killerton

KILVER COURT
Kilver Street, Shepton Mallet,
Somerset, BA4 5NF
Tel: 01749 340410
www.kilvercourt.com/
secret-gardens

FEATURED GARDENS

KINGSTON LACY
Wimborne Minster, Dorset,
BH21 4EA
Tel: 01202 883402
www.nationaltrust.org.uk/
kingston-lacy

KINGSTON MAURWARD
GARDENS
Dorchester, Dorset, DT2 8PY
Tel: 01305 215000
www.kmc.ac.uk/gardens

KNIGHTSHAYES
Bolham, Tiverton, EX16 7RQ
Tel: 01884 254665
www.nationaltrust.org.uk/
knightshayes

KNOLL GARDENS
Stapehill Road, Hampreston,
Wimborne, BH21 7ND
Tel: 01202 873931
www.knollgardens.co.uk

LAMORRAN
Upper Castle Road, Saint Mawes,
Truro, Cornwall, TR2 5BZ
Tel: 01326 270800
www.lamorrangardens.co.uk

LANHYDROCK
Bodmin, Cornwall, PL30 5AD
Tel: 01208 265950
www.nationaltrust.org.uk/
lanhydrock

LOST GARDENS OF HELIGAN
Pentewan, Saint Austell, Cornwall,
PL26 6EN
Tel: 01726 845100
www.heligan.com

MAPPERTON
Mapperton, Beaminster, Dorset,
DT8 3NR
Tel: 01308 862645
www.mapperton.com

MARWOOD HILL
Barnstaple, North Devon,
EX31 4EB
Tel: 01271 342528
www.marwoodhillgarden.co.uk

MINTERNE GARDENS
Minterne Magna, Dorchester,
Dorset, DT2 7AU
Tel: 01300 341370
www.minterne.co.uk/mjs/gardens

MONTACUTE HOUSE
Montacute, Yeovil, Somerset,
TA15 6XP
Tel: 01935 823289
www.nationaltrust.org.uk/
montacute-house

OVERBECK'S
Sharpitor, Devon, TQ8 8LW
Tel: 01548 842893
www.nationaltrust.org.uk/
overbecks

PAIGNTON ZOO & BOTANICAL
GARDENS
Totnes Road, Paignton, Devon,
TQ4 7EU
Tel: 08444 742222
www.paigntonzoo.org.uk

PINETUM PARK & PINELODGE
GARDENS
Holmbush, Saint Austell,
Cornwall, PL25 3RQ
Tel: 01726 73500
www.pinetumpark.com

RHS ROSEMOOR
Rosemoor Garden, Torrington,
EX38 8PH
Tel: 01805 624067
www.rhs.org.uk/gardens/
rosemoor

SALTRAM HOUSE
Plympton, Plymouth, Devon,
PL7 1UH
Tel: 01752 333503
www.nationaltrust.org.uk/saltram

THE GARDEN HOUSE
Buckland Monachorum,
Yelverton, Devon, PL20 7LQ
Tel: 01822 854769
www.thegardenhouse.org.uk

TREBAH
Trebah Garden Trust, Mawnan
Smith, Falmouth, TR11 5JZ
Tel: 01326 252200
www.trebahgarden.co.uk

TRELISSICK
Feock, Truro, Cornwall, TR3 6QL
Tel: 01872 862090
www.nationaltrust.org.uk/
trelissick

TRENGWAINTON
Madron, Penzance, Cornwall,
TR20 8RZ
Tel: 01736 363148
www.nationaltrust.org.uk/
trengwainton-garden

TRESCO ABBEY GARDENS
Tresco, Isles of Scilly, TR24 0QQ
Tel: 01720 424105
www.tresco.co.uk/enjoying/
abbey-garden

TREWITHEN
Grampound Road, Truro,
Cornwall, TR2 4DD
Tel: 01726 883647
www.trewithengardens.co.uk

TYNTESFIELD
Wraxall, Bristol, BS48 1NX
Tel: 08448 004966
tyntesfield@nationaltrust.org.uk

UNIVERSITY OF BRISTOL
BOTANIC GARDEN
Hollybush Lane, Bristol, BS9 1JB
Tel: 01173 314906
www.bristol.ac.uk/botanic-garden

THE MAP OF GARDENS

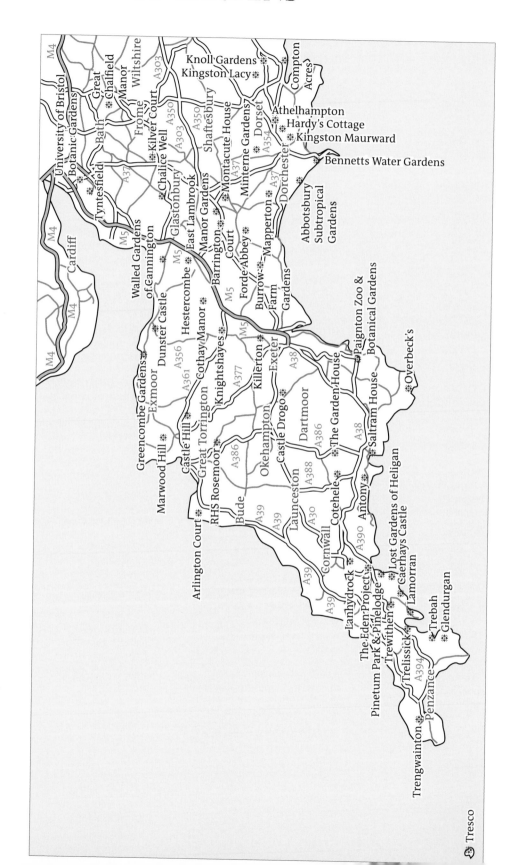

❀ ABBOTSBURY SUBTROPICAL GARDENS

Established in 1765 by the first Countess of Ilchester, this 30-acre (12 hectare) Grade I listed garden sits in a sheltered fold of hills that rise directly behind Chesil Beach. Abbotsbury's proximity to the sea means frosts are infrequent or seldom prolonged. Consequently, one of the most successful collections of tender subtropical plants in Britain has been established here in south Dorset.

The feeling that this is no ordinary English garden is evident from the moment you glimpse the red tin-roofed, colonial-style garden restaurant that greets you on arrival. In summer, surrounded by a jungle-like fecundity of foliage and flowers, a setting such as this would have felt familiar to government officials administering some far-flung outpost of the British Empire 100 years ago. South African strelitizias, Australian callistemon with brilliant crimson bottlebrush-like flowers, New Zealand cordylines, ligularias from China, with big, fleshy triangular leaves and tall spikes of yellow flowers, brugmansias from South America, their giant, pendulous, trumpet-shaped flowers swaying gently in the slightest breeze and Mexican hesper palms are all here to be admired.

Considerable restoration work has taken place since the Burn's Day storm of January 1990, which wreaked havoc throughout much of the garden, and hundreds of new and exotic plants have been introduced into a series of exciting garden landscapes created for the twenty-first century and changing climatic conditions. ▶

Victorian Walled Garden

❁ ABBOTSBURY SUBTROPICAL GARDENS

◀ The garden is now a mixture of formal and informal, with a charming Victorian walled garden and a spectacular woodland valley garden. Within the valley, Abbotsbury's famous camellia grove has been supplemented with many new camellia cultivars and fine specimens of magnolia and rhododendron have been planted alongside – all of which provide a riot of colour from March right through until June.

As spring flowering begins to wane, in the moist, rich soil margins of the valley stream, which is crossed by red-painted Oriental-style bridges, tree ferns, giant-leaved Brazilian rhubarb, candelabra primulas,

rheums, rodgersias and pure white drifts of flowering arum lilies provide the perfect cooling accompaniment to summer.

Recently created is the new Southern Hemisphere Garden which houses a National Collection of Hoheria, a beautiful genus similar to mallow with masses of white flowers in early summer.

One of the greatest successes of the past ten years at Abbotsbury has been the development of the Mediterranean Bank. On this hot, sunny, free-draining slope, plants such as agapanthus and watsonia freely flower all summer long and in places they have even become naturalised.

◀ Spring Woodland Garden

Colonial-style garden restaurant

❀ ANTONY

Antony House was built for Sir William Carew in 1724 and replaced a Tudor mansion that had been home to the Carew family since 1432. The family (now Carew Pole) still live here and take great pride and care in continuing to maintain and enhance the gardens.

In 1792, Humphry Repton was invited to Antony, and his advice, presented in one of his famous 'red books' (still in the family possession), was in part taken up. Some, but not all, of the formal walled gardens close to the house were cleared and replaced by a naturalistic parkland landscape with long vistas and informal tree plantings, a remnant of which is a large multi-limbed American black walnut

Juglans nigra, which survives to this day on the main lawn. This mixture of formality and informality is evident to such an extent that Antony can justifiably be said to have two gardens. The formal garden close to the house, amounting to 35 acres (14 hectares), is owned and managed by the National Trust, whereas the woodland garden, otherwise known as the 'Wilderness' and covering a further 60 acres (24 hectares), is run by the Carew Pole Garden Trust.

There are some features which pre-date Repton's involvement, including the terrace, red-brick circular dovecote and groves of evergreen oak *Quercus Ilex*, planted in the 1760s to frame the vista from the house to the River Lynher. ▶

Antony House

Japanese-style Garden ▶

◀ Today, white-flowering rugosa roses, lavender and vigorous drifts of *Nepeta* 'Six Hills Giant' fringe the terraces, below which lie several delightful and intimate spaces, including a Japanese garden with pool, Japanese maples and both blue- and white-flowering wisteria, created by Sir John Carew Pole in the early years of the twentieth century. Just beyond lies a scented Summer Garden and Knot Garden, developed in 1983 by Lady Mary Carew Pole and bordered by dense yew hedging. Near the old tennis court, a close-clipped yew topiary cone provides inspiration for William Pye's 1995 'Watercone' sculpture. Planted close to some of the original garden walls not removed by Repton is Antony's National Collection of daylilies *Hemerocallis*, which currently contains over 600 cultivars.

Elsewhere, avenues of *Magnolia grandiflora* 'Exmouth' and *Magnolia x soulangeana* bring spring colour to this garden, which is further enhanced across the lawns in the Wilderness where, in this more typical Cornish garden mature rhododendrons, magnolias and over 2,000 varieties of camellia, including Antony's National Collection of *Camellia japonica* cultivars, are to be found.

Summer Garden

❀ ARLINGTON COURT

The combination of a mild, damp climate and acid soil provides the perfect Devon home for a wide range of ericaceous plants, especially rhododendrons, which grow to tree-like proportions in Arlington's Pleasure Grounds. This late eighteenth- and early nineteenth-century picturesque landscape has a Wilderness Pond at its centre, the placid waters of which reflect the tower of nearby St James' church.

Attractive as this undoubtedly is, what makes a visit to Arlington Court essential for anyone with even a passing interest in period garden design is its faithful recreation of a style that was at the height of fashion during the reign of Queen Victoria. Influences from this period are seen throughout Arlington, be it in the avenue of monkey-puzzle trees that line the West Drive or the obelisk in the south-east park erected to commemorate the Golden Jubilee in 1887. However, it is in the formal layout and plantings of the Victorian Garden where the horticultural clock really has been turned back.

Originally developed by Arlington owner Sir Bruce Chichester in what had been the old garden enclosures of an earlier Tudor manor house, the Victorian Garden has in recent years undergone restoration by the National Trust and stands today as a testament to their skill, knowledge and understanding of this particular period in garden history. ▶

Victorian Garden

◀ From the entrance gate a pair of ornamental herons, each with a wriggling eel in their mouth, flank the lower terrace slate steps that ascend a central pathway. As the steps are climbed a series of terraces are revealed, each with its own features. At first, the plantings are of banks of brightly coloured Japanese azaleas. These give way to lawns with a circular pool and stone fountain encircled by vibrantly coloured bedding begonias. Alongside are crescent-shaped beds, also full of brightly coloured annuals and stone urns planted with variegated agaves. Giving height to the terrace are arched trellises planted with honeysuckle. The terrace above has circular basket beds filled with colourful annuals and ironwork frames supporting climbing *Cobaea scandens*.

Overlooking all is a conservatory, built to replace the original glasshouses that stretched right along the back wall and containing a selection of tender flowering plants from Australia, New Zealand and South Africa. Immediately outside the conservatory, herbaceous borders, designed in a semi-formal pattern to continue the Victorian theme, flank the gravel pathway that leads to a door opening into a 1-acre (0.4-hectare) walled kitchen garden.

◀ Walled Kitchen Garden

Conservatory and terrace

✺ ATHELHAMPTON HOUSE GARDENS

Given his lifelong fascination with architecture and stone masonry, it is no suprise that Thomas Hardy was a frequent visitor to Athelhampton House near Dorchester, Dorset. Dating from 1485, its Great Hall is a magnificent example of early Tudor architecture with surviving heraldic glass, linenfold panelling and carved roof timbers. In 1891, in front of the house, owner Alfred Carte de Lafontaine commissioned Francis Inigo Thomas to design and build a series of formal ham stone court gardens in the Elizabethan style. The project took until 1899 to complete. Today, the gardens are Grade I listed and have won the prestigious HHA 'Garden of the Year Award'.

The most famous garden is The Great Court, which contains twelve striking pyramid-shaped topiary yew trees. Planted not only to echo the stone obelisks bordering the nearby raised terrace walk, they were originally intended to punctuate the corners of formal rose beds, now long gone. Today the yew pyramids stand some 30 feet (9 metres) tall and dominate the court without any need for further embellishment other than a central lily pool and fountain. Standing at each end of the terrace are matching pavilions, also designed by Francis Inigo Thomas. ▸

Coronet Garden   The Pyramid Garden ▸

❀ ATHELHAMPTON HOUSE GARDENS

◀ Beyond the Great Court is the Corona, a circular garden surrounded by stone walls shaped like a crown and placed against a backdrop of clipped yew hedging and shaded by the level boughs of ancient cedars. Within the circular crown, quadrant borders of herbs, New Zealand phormiums and shrubs help to soften the surrounding formality.

Further gardens include the Private Garden, Octagonal Pond and Long Canal, which in summer are studded with flowering water lilies. Water is a recurring theme at Athelhampton with fountains and pools featuring throughout most of the garden compartments, which all link together, thereby creating a labyrinth of

rooms that eventually leads to the River Piddle, the natural boundary to the garden. Here, raised boardwalks extend along the embankment to join paths which eventually lead to a fifteenth-century circular dovecote on the lawn facing the west wing of the house. The dovecote is still home to a colony of beautiful white fantail doves.

Balancing the hard landscaping is an ever-present background of woodland, and behind the Great Court a circular grove of pleached limes adds further to the architectural interest. Where softer planting occurs it is low key and sophisticated and predominantly built around bulbs, roses and climbers.

Pyramid Garden

✤ BARRINGTON COURT

In 1917 Gertrude Jekyll was in her late seventies, had poor eyesight and was approaching the end of her career when she was commissioned by National Trust tenant Col Arthur Lyle (of the sugar refining company) to design a planting scheme for his new garden at Barrington Court. Despite these problems, Jekyll managed to produce some of the best designs of her career and the planting schemes adopted today by family descendants of Col Lyle in this Grade II listed garden are still based upon her original ideas.

Barrington Court is a fine Tudor manor house dating back to 1538 and was one of the first houses acquired by the National Trust in 1907. It was originally surrounded by a medieval deer park, and in the seventeenth century a formal garden was created, although most of this disappeared when the Arts and Crafts-style garden planted by Jekyll was created in the twentieth century. There are still long avenues of mature trees approaching the house and the remains of a rectangular raised parterre predate Jekyll, but Barrington is today best known for having one of the best preserved examples of her work in Britain. ▶

Rose border

◄ The main flower gardens are in Hidcote-style with a series of 'garden rooms', each separated by walls and entered through silver weathered oak doors and traversed via delightful brick-patterned pathways, fringed with lavender and catmint. Rooms include The White Garden, a circular design growing white-flowering annual and perennial plants including phlox, alyssum and cosmos and silver-leaved foliage plants such as stachys in the style of the White Garden at Sissinghurst.

The Lily Garden has a rectangular lawn and central water lily pool, surrounded by raised beds planted in a vibrant and bold mix of hot colours, including oranges, reds and yellows. Here deciduous fragrant azaleas, ranging in colour from flame red to salmon pink, combine with orange early flowering daylilies *Hemerocallis sp.* Other beds include peach-coloured alstroemeria, red *Crocosmia* 'Lucifer' and yellow hypericum. While the present-day designs may not be exactly the plants recommended by Jekyll, the colour schemes are, and what comes through is her peerless talent for blending and graduating colours in a way that looks natural and seamless.

There is also a rose and iris garden and a large kitchen garden with gravel paths laid out in a square, with a central fountain surrounded by vegetables, soft fruit and fruit trees and beyond the moat, which borders the garden walls, is a cider orchard.

◄ A series of garden rooms
(Image courtesy of Michael Clarke, Flickr)

Dahlia borders

BENNETTS WATER GARDENS

The 8-acre (3.2-hectare) gardens at Bennetts Water Gardens, located on the south coast near Weymouth, hold the National Plant Collection (Plant Heritage formerly NCCPG) of *Nymphaea* – hardy water lilies which flower from May to September. In total, there are more than 100 hardy cultivars at Bennetts, all grown in a series of outdoor ponds and lakes with some tender specimens housed within a small tropical glasshouse; together they make one of the most outstanding displays of water lilies in Britain. A main feature of the garden is a blue painted Japanese-style bridge built in 1999 to celebrate the centenary of Claude Monet's famous work *Water Lily Pond*.

The garden is the creation of the Bennett family and in particular Norman Bennett, who started growing water lilies in 1959 in a disused clay pit formerly belonging to Putton Brickworks. His success with these aquatic beauties was immediate and soon he was not only growing them, but had started a water lily nursery and was exporting plants worldwide. As such, Bennetts is today one of the oldest water lily nurseries in Europe. Norman was also a founder member of the International Water Lily Society, and although now retired his family still run the garden and the nursery and he continues to share his great knowledge of water lilies with fellow enthusiasts. ▸

Monet-style bridge

The Imperial Gazebo ▸

❀ BENNETTS WATER GARDENS

◀ Many of the original water lilies planted by Norman Bennett came from the nursery in France that supplied Claude Monet's garden in Giverny. Frenchman Joseph Latour-Marliac is considered the father of water lily hybridising and created over 100 new cultivars in the late 1800s and early 1900s. Some of these were the varieties that Monet painted, including *Nymphaea* 'Laydekeri Rosea' and *Nymphaea odorata* 'Sulphurea grandiflora' and now make up part of the collection on display in Bennetts Water Gardens today.

Grass pathways lead you past a series of themed ponds and lakes, such as the White Lily Pond, New Lily Pond and Orfe Pond where The Imperial Gazebo, located on a peninsula, provides beautiful views across the water. Surrounding the lakes are collections of wetland plants, native trees, palms, cordylines and wildflowers. The garden is a 'Site of Nature Conservation Interest' and home to an abundance of wildlife, which includes many species of dragonflies.

There is also a museum on site which tells the fascinating story of the site from the brickworks and clay pits in 1859 right through to the water gardens of the present day.

Bennetts holds the National Collection of water lilies

BURROW FARM GARDENS

When Mary and John Benger moved to Burrow Farm in 1959 it was a typical dairy farm with every scrap of half decent land given over to pasture for the cows.

Initially, while John was concentrating on the farm and building up the herd, Mary was busy raising a family of four. However, even then she knew that at some point she would create a garden around the family home.

Eventually Mary began to actively search for somewhere to start her garden. The only area not given over to farming was an old Roman clay pit, so in 1963, beneath an ancient field maple tree, she and her four young children began to clear decades of bramble growth in preparation.

Eventually Mary's garden out-grew the Roman clay pit and she began to 'pinch' corners of pasture from John. Such was her success that by 1974 she had created 4 acres (1.6 hectares) of garden, and in the following year Burrow Farm Garden opened to the public for the first time under the National Garden Scheme. John retired from farming in 1983 and from then on the garden developed in leaps and bounds.

Today, the Roman clay pit is a woodland garden comprised of mature trees under-planted with rhododendrons, azaleas and other spring-flowering shrubs. ▶

Burrow Farm Gardens

❀ BURROW FARM GARDENS

◀ At the bottom of the slope formed from the clay pit is an extensive bog garden full of large-leaved foliage plants such as the American skunk cabbage *Lysichitum americanum,* rheums and rodgersias, candelabra primulas and native wild flowers, including swathes of bluebells.

Elsewhere there is a pergola walk, which in summer is a picture with its intimate mix of old-fashioned roses and climbing *Akebia quinata.* There are also extensive and well-designed herbaceous borders, and around a new house, built in 1990 to replace the original bungalow, courtyard and terrace gardens have been developed;

the latter being comprised of a rather formal layout with strong architectural features softened by cottage-garden-style planting. A rill garden was created for the Millennium and here water runs through the centre of colour-themed plantings and into a pool overlooked by a stone gazebo. In recent years an Azalea Glade has been added, and to celebrate fifty years since John and Mary arrived at Burrow Farm an Anniversary Garden too. Here ornamental grasses wave gently above a sunken path, surrounded by a profusion of pink, blue and purple-flowering perennials, which look especially good during late summer and autumn.

◀ Bog Garden with *Candelabra primulas*   Azalea Glade

❀ CAERHAYS CASTLE GARDEN

Few gardens in Britain can rival the idyllic location of Caerhays Castle Garden in Cornwall. It is approached from Porthluney Cove, a secluded south-facing sun trap, where the sea breaks on a silver-grained beach. If that is not enough to whet your appetite, then perhaps the indisputable fact that this is one of the greatest spring gardens in the UK will.

At its heart is a castle furnished with battlements, turrets and towers in a way that would even put Caernarfon Castle to the test if it were not for the fact that Caerhays was only built in 1807. Principally a romantic illusion, it casts a wistful eye back to the age of chivalry and 'Knights of Old'; but do not dismiss it too quickly, for its architect was John Nash of Buckingham Palace and Brighton Pavilion fame and Caerhays Castle is undeniably spectacular, as well as being one of very few Nash-built castles still standing.

Principally a woodland garden of 120 acres (49 hectares), Caerhays has Grade II English Heritage listing, is home to National Collections of Magnolia and Podocarpus and contains seventy-eight champion trees (the biggest in the UK). Not only that, it also has fine collections of mature rhododendrons and camellias. ▶

Caerhays Castle

Porthluney Cove ▶

◀ The origins of this superb garden can be traced back to one man – John Charles Williams MP – who gave up parliamentary life and turned his back on London society in 1896 to concentrate on developing a garden on his family's estate at Caerhays.

'J. C.' (as he became known) was inspired by the exciting botanical discoveries which British plant collectors were making in the Far East. So when Chelsea nurserymen Veitch & Sons asked him to grow seeds which had been collected by plant hunters like E. H. Wilson and George Forrest, he greeted the request with unbounded enthusiasm. From 1900 until his death in 1939, J. C. grew literally hundreds of rhododendrons, camellias, magnolias, maples and other Asian plants that had never been grown in Britain before. Not only that, he began to hybridise species, producing superb new garden cultivars in the process, including what has become today the world-famous range of *Camellia x williamsii* hybrids.

Don't worry if all this history leaves you dry, I guarantee the plants and garden won't. While Caerhays is wild, weedy and woody in places, that is its charm, and out of all of this springs one of the most remarkable plant collections in the British Isles.

Magnolia doltsopa and rhododendron

❧ THE WALLED GARDENS OF CANNINGTON

Located in the village of Cannington, near Bridgwater in Somerset, The Walled Gardens of Cannington lie within the grounds of a medieval priory, the remains of which make for a fine backdrop to this fascinating garden. Cannington Priory (later to become Cannington Court) was first established in 1138 as a place of worship for Benedictine nuns, and was home to the daughters of many of Somerset's leading families. The nuns tended gardens surrounding the priory, so there has been gardening and horticultural activity on this site for almost 900 years. In 1919, Cannington Court became the location for the Somerset College of Agriculture and Horticulture, which in turn became Cannington College merging with Bridgwater College in 2004. Throughout this time, students have learned the basics and best practices of horticulture and used the grounds to develop a series of varied and inspirational gardens. Since 2004, significant investment has been put into redeveloping the Walled Gardens and they were officially reopened to the public by HRH the Earl of Wessex Prince Edward in 2009. ▸

Tropical House

❋ THE WALLED GARDENS OF CANNINGTON

◀ The gardens include both classic and contemporary themes, including 'hot' herbaceous borders, which are full of vibrant red, orange and yellow-flowering plants and a blue garden, where cool pastel shades surround a modern water feature designed by a previous college student, providing the perfect contrast to the brighter colours elsewhere. There is also an Australasian Garden and a sub-tropical walk where Chusan palms *Trachycarpus fortunei,* large-leaved Japanese bananas *Musa basjoo,* Canary Island *Echium wildprettii* and *E. pininana* and South African agapanthus show just how sheltered and warm this red-stone, walled garden really is. It is worth considering that when the nuns first started gardening here some 900 years ago, most of these geographical locations were unknown to western civilisation, and in the case of Australasia would remain so for a further 600 years!

A series of show gardens, a botanical glasshouse growing arid, subtropical and tropical plants, and a potager (an ornamental kitchen garden designed to be both productive and aesthetically pleasing) showcasing vegetables, fruit and companion plants helpful against pests and diseases, all add to the diversity of this unique garden that works on three levels. It ensures the continuation of a garden legacy that stretches back to the medieval period, it provides a dynamic learning environment for current-day horticultural students and it is a garden of real beauty and interest that all visitors will enjoy.

◀ Blue Garden

Echium wildprettii

❁ CASTLE DROGO

This Grade II listed garden, with its dramatic views over Dartmoor and the Teign Gorge, surrounds the last 'castle' to be built in England. Begun in 1910, this formidable looking but fantastical granite-walled neo-Norman fortress scowling down from its exposed rocky prominence was designed by Edwin Lutyens for Julius Drewe, the owner of the Home and Colonial chain of grocery stores.

Gertrude Jekyll suggested that a series of terraced gardens should cascade down from the building, similar to the style found below Powis Castle. However, Drewe felt this would diminish the grandeur of the building, favouring instead a design that kept any formal garden landscape at arm's length with 'untamed wilderness' of pine-studded moorland the castle's closer companion.

The plans for the garden were eventually drawn up by George Dillistone, with some input by Lutyens, with the main gardens positioned across the drive to the north of the castle and accessed by a gravel terrace. Today, the steep valley below this terrace is planted with evergreen oaks *Quercus ilex*, sheltering a woodland garden with extensive collections of spring-flowering rhododendrons, camellias, magnolias, lichen-encrusted cherries, cornus and maples. ▸

Azaleas and maples fringe the pathways
(*Image courtesy of Matthew, Flickr*)

Terrace Gardens ▸

◀ Beyond the terrace, the formal gardens are entered through a timbered gateway. Like the castle, the gardens are full of strong architectural lines and surrounded by walls of yew almost as thick as the castle walls. Even so, there is little more shelter here than if they had been clinging to the skirts of the castle. At 1,000 feet (304 metres) above sea level they rank among the highest and most exposed gardens managed by the National Trust. Laid out on three main terraces, the lower terrace includes a sunken rose garden. Julius Drewe had this established for his wife Frances as roses were her favourite flowers. It is designed in a chequerboard style with twenty-four square and rectangular beds set within a lawn and planted with old-fashioned and modern shrubs, and floribunda roses. The terrace above is planted with herbaceous borders full of textured plantings including crocosmia, lychnis, campanula, iris and kniphofia, interspersed with slate-edged gravel pathways that follow a geometric Indian pattern seen by Lutyens in Delhi. At each corner, cast-iron framed pergolas are clothed in Persian ironwoods *Persica parrotia*. It is, however, the top terrace that holds the biggest surprise, for here, surrounded by yew hedging, is a magnificent circular lawn, the perfect place to play croquet, just as long as the ball does not blow away!

Persica parrotia

❊ CASTLE HILL GARDENS

Situated in the rolling hills of North Devon is Castle Hill, the estate of the Earl and Countess of Arran. At the heart of the estate, nestling in a broad horseshoe of low hills, is an elegant Palladian house originally built in 1730 for the 1st Earl of Fortescue, a direct ancestor of the current Earl and Countess.

Sweeping away from the house, a stunning eighteenth-century Grade I listed landscape garden and park has changed little since its creation. A series of grass terraces, statuary and close-clipped columnar Irish yews *Taxus baccata* 'Fastigiata' flow down to a tributary of the River Mole, along which are several carefully positioned lakes and cascades. From here, the eye is drawn to a triumphal arch that stands majestically at the furthest point of a tree-lined vista and perfectly balances the view back to the house and a sham castle, complete with cannon, which dominates the skyline directly above. The climb to the castle is steep but it is worth it, for on a clear day the views to Exmoor, Dartmoor and Lundy Island in the Bristol Channel are breathtaking.

It is from the castle that one also gets the best overview of the woodland garden, which winds sinuously away from the house through a sheltered valley protected by belts of mature beech, larch and some fine old spruce. ▸

Millenium Garden

✣ CASTLE HILL GARDENS

◄ Covering 50 acres (20 hectares), much of the shrub and tree planting within the woodland garden has taken place since the Burn's Day storm of January 1990, which destroyed up to 50 per cent of the original plants.

From March onwards, the valley sides are beautifully shrouded in white, pink and red-flowering camellias, rhododendrons and magnolias, beneath which carpets of snowdrops, narcissi and bluebells perform in succession. The climax to the spring season comes when drifts of Ghent and Kurume hybrid azaleas fill the valley with sweet fragrance.

Recognising that summer is an important time in any garden, the current Earl and Countess have created a Millennium summer garden to the east of the house. Designed by Chelsea Gold Medallist Xa Tollemache, and comprising a delightful water sculpture by Giles Rayner, it features large borders edged with box and lavender and filled with white and pastel-shaded herbaceous plants and bulbs. To give height and structure to the garden, a number of topiary-domed evergreen oaks *Quercus ilex* have been included, each one skirted by scrolls of clipped *Viburnum tinus*.

◄ View from the Sham Castle

Autumn at Castle Hill

✿ CHALICE WELL GARDENS

Nestling in the Vale of Avalon, this mystical, tranquil and beautiful sanctuary garden is situated at the foot of Glastonbury Tor, around an ancient holy well which is believed to have been a place of pilgrimage for over 2,000 years and the location where Joseph of Arimathea washed the chalice cup used at the Last Supper of Christ. Surrounding the well are ferns and ivies thriving in the dappled shade cast by several yew trees. The clear spring waters that feed the well also flow through the gardens and provide the inspiration for several features, including pools, cascades and rills located within the beautifully landscaped World Peace Garden.

This is not a plantsman's garden, nor a garden full of important botanical collections; however it admirably fulfils one of the main reasons for creating any garden. It provides a place of sanctuary, somewhere to recharge our batteries and a delightfully quiet space where each and every one of us can come to terms with whatever life may choose to throw at us.

Entry to the garden is beneath a pergola, which in early summer drips with white wisteria, climbing roses and hanging baskets full of colourful bedding and trailing plants. ▶

Chalice Well in spring

Red Spring ▶
(Image courtesy of Angela Sessions, Flickr)

◀ From here one enters the lower gardens and the Vesica Pool, which is fed by a free-form cascade that swirls the entering water in a mesmerising figure-of-eight motion, all set in a rockery planted with dwarf conifers and alpine plants. From the garden and the adjacent meadow there are delightful views of Glastonbury Tor, Chalice Hill and the Somerset Levels. Ancient yew trees, known as the 'guardians of the well', and believed to be centuries old, provide coolness and shade on hot sunny days and shelter from the cold winds that blow from the levels in winter.

With the renewed interest in healing plants, a physic garden containing over 100 different medicinal plant species has been established and includes arnica, echinacea, mugwort, valerian, evening primrose and sweet cicely. Chalice Well is a garden of many 'rooms' or outdoor spaces, each with its own theme or characteristics. One of the loveliest spaces is The Sanctuary, where mellow-coloured south-facing stone walls soak up the sun before radiating warmth back on to garden seats positioned amid swathes of white-flowering cosmos. There is also a wild flower meadow, which in spring is bedecked in swathes of daffodils, a living willow maze and an orchard containing several local Somerset varieties of apple.

Herbaceous borders

✿ COMPTON ACRES

Compton Acres is one of the finest privately owned gardens in England. Situated near the Channel coast just west of Bournemouth, it boasts a unique collection of five striking gardens – an Italian Garden, Japanese Garden, Rock and Water Garden, Heather Garden and Woodland Garden. The latter is set in a valley of mature pine trees, beneath which many ornamental shrubs including rhododendrons and camellias have been planted. From within the garden there are spectacular views of Poole Harbour, Brownsea Island and across the sea to Dorset's Purbeck Hills.

The garden was created in the 1920s by Thomas William Simpson, an entrepreneur who made his fortune through the manufacture of margarine. Simpson was strongly influenced by the Arts & Crafts movement, and Compton Acres is widely regarded as one of the most outstanding gardens constructed in Britain during that period.

In the past ten years the gardens have undergone extensive refurbishment and restoration, with designers and gardeners using modern horticultural techniques and modern plant cultivars to ensure all-year-round interest. During this period, over 1,000 new plant varieties have been added to the collection. The new design takes the form of a necklace of separate gardens, each with its own unique style and each providing different interest, plants and colour. ▸

Japanese Garden with azaleas

◀ Perhaps the most famous feature at Compton Acres is the Italian Garden. Here visitors can enjoy terraces bordered by stone balustrades and clipped evergreens while gazing upon a large formal pool with fountains, display beds planted with colourful bedding and bulb schemes and a whole host of statues, including one of Bacchus, the Greco-Roman God of winemaking, set within his own domed temple.

In spring the Woodland Garden is a delight, with paths leading to painted rustic bridges that cross tumbling streams fringed by vibrant coloured and fragrant deciduous azaleas. Also, in spring, the Rock Garden comes into its own when over 2,000 dwarf spring bulbs begin to flower. The Heather Garden, which is normally at its most colourful in winter, is currently undergoing further restoration, including the planting of new dwarf conifers and heaths.

Compton Acres' Japanese Garden is widely recognised as being one of the best in Britain. It provides the very essence of a style of tea garden found in and around Kyoto on the main Japanese island of Honshu. There is a thatched summerhouse and at the garden's centre a vermillion painted teahouse, constructed to an authentic design and draped in Japanese wisteria *Wisteria sinensis*.

◀ Italian-style formal pool with foutains
(*Image courtesy of Paul Lancaster, Flickr*)

Italian Garden

✤ COTEHELE

Home to the Edgcumbe family from the fourteenth century until 1947, when the National Trust took up stewardship, Cotehele is positioned high above the Tamar valley and has far-reaching views eastwards across the River Tamar, the architectural splendour of Calstock viaduct and the bare expanses of Dartmoor beyond.

The garden, which was laid out to its present design in the nineteenth century, covers 17 acres (6.9 hectares) and is in fact two gardens wvithin one, an upper formal garden that surrounds the house and a lower wild valley garden, which descends a steep wooded combe to Sir Richard Edgcumbe's chapel and Cotehele quay's eighteenth-century limekilns.

At the entrance to the property is a magnificent fifteenth-century tithe barn (now tea rooms) with an undulating roof, which seems to reflect the surrounding rolling countryside. Beyond lies the sixteenth-century Tudor house, complete with tower and battlements. To the eastern front of the house, its walls softened with clematis, wisteria and *Magnolia grandiflora*, is a series of formal stone terraces, part lawn part flower borders and planted with pastel shades and silver foliage. Stone archways and cobbled courtyards, bordered by *Camellia* 'Cornish snow' and myrtle, open out to sloping meadows covered in spring with drifts of narcissi, their flowers varying in colour from paper white to orange yellow across twenty-seven varieties. ▸

Cotehele

Entrance into Upper Walled Garden ▸

◀ Paths bordered with cork oaks *Quercus suber* lead through a white-painted entrance gate shaded by boughs of a large New Zealand tea tree *Leptospermum scoparium* and into the Upper Walled Garden, where sloping lawns run to a central lily pool fed by a babbling rivulet. Against the walls, hot and bright herbaceous borders bring sunshine to the garden even on a cloudy day. Yew hedging separates this garden from a cut-flower garden and apple orchard stocked with West Country varieties.

The top path leads back past clouds of sweet-scented *Erica arborea var. alpina* to a stone balustrade below the eastern terrace, where there are delightful views down the combe to a medieval dovecote and stewpond, once purely functional now beautiful follies in the surrounding landscape. From here paths follow tumbling streams down through the combe, which in true Cornish fashion is stocked with large Cornish Red rhododendrons (or as they are otherwise known across the border 'Devon Pink') and a wonderful collection of tender spring-flowering shrubs and foliage plants, all shaded beneath rare Mexican pines *Pinus patula*, tree ferns and Chusan palms *Trachycarpus fortunei*.

Medieval Dovecot

❀ COTHAY MANOR

Five miles west of Wellington, hidden in the high-banked lanes of Somerset and idyllically positioned upon the banks of the River Tone, is perhaps one of the most beautiful properties in the West Country – Cothay Manor. Built at the end of the Wars of the Roses in 1485, Cothay has remained virtually unchanged for 500 years. Adjacent to the medieval manor house are 12 acres (4.8 hectares) of superb gardens, which appear at first glance to be integral to the property, however they were only laid out in the 1920s and have been painstakingly restored over the past twenty years by Cothay owners Mary-Anne Robb and her husband Alastair. In fact, they not only restored but also cleverly redesigned and replanted within their original infrastructure, which includes a 200-yard-long (183-metre) 'yew-walk' – a seventeenth-century promenade interspersed with 'conversation arbours'.

Positioned off the promenade are a series of compartments or garden rooms each with a different theme, such as in the Bishop's Room, where an intricately designed box parterre is offset by borders of colour, which in late spring includes red peonies, lilac and purple alliums and 'Ribena-coloured' *Papaver orientale* 'Patty's Plum'. ▶

Cothay Manor

◀ Elsewhere, there are herbaceous borders, a cottage garden, cherry garden and a beautiful white garden.

A good eye for form and colour and a great knowledge of plants and their requirements is evident everywhere at Cothay, and the Robbs have managed to achieve a comfortable balance between exuberance and restraint, while at the same time they have not shied away from repeating a theme where it appears particularly successful. Their use of complementing purples, lilacs and greys alongside the house walls is unusual but works supremely well.

One of the finest sights in spring at Cothay is the 'Walk of the Unicorn' a 70-yard-long (64-metre) avenue of pruned *Robinia pseudoacacia* 'Umbraculifera', underplanted with *Nepeta* 'Six Hills Giant' and enhanced by thousands of white tulips, which are also allowed to march out across the rest of the garden.

Forming a fabulous backdrop to the gardens is an arboretum, where in the past twenty years specimen trees, shrubs and spring bulbs have been planted around a small lake. Near the fast-flowing water of the River Tone is a bog garden planted with azaleas and drifts of primulas. Along with the surrounding flower meadows, the abundance of water at Cothay makes for important wildlife habitats for insects and over forty different species of birds.

◀ Herbaceous borders full of colour

Walk of the Unicorn

❊ DUNSTER CASTLE AND GARDENS

Home to the Luttrell family from 1376, Dunster Castle was given to the National Trust exactly 600 years later in 1976 by Col Sir Walter Luttrell. During that 600-year period the castle went through several transformations. The building which greets visitors today, with its warm red sandstone battlements and towers set high upon a rocky outcrop, owes much to the work carried out in the 1860s by architect Anthony Salvin.

Likewise, the gardens and grounds have seen many changes over the years. Records from 1543 refer to a walled kitchen garden east of Dunster church, however nothing remains of this today. In 1755, Henry Fownes Luttrell created a large deer park and commissioned pleasure grounds below the castle. These were laid out in the Picturesque Landscape style of the day and included romantic bridges, theatrical arches, ruined folly 'eye-catchers' and artificial cascades. Much of this can still be seen and a series of footpaths take in the most dramatic features, including the River Avill, alongside which many rare and tender exotics, planted by Alys Luttrell in the 1920s, now thrive within the valley's warm microclimate, enhanced by its close proximity to the sea. Here you will find large specimens of rhododendron, camellia, eucryphia, big-leaved hydrangeas, Brazilian rhubarb *Gunnera manicata,* hostas and ferns. ▸

Bananas on the Castle Terrace

Dunster Castle ▸

✤ DUNSTER CASTLE AND GARDENS

◀ Relating to the earlier Victorian era, the series of formal gardens and terraces that wind their way up the rocky outcrop to skirt the castle walls, before spilling out into the Keep Garden, contain perhaps the most ornamental collection of plants at Dunster. The Keep Garden is positioned at the highest point in the immediate landscape and offers fine views of Exmoor, the Quantocks and the Bristol Channel. At its centre is an elliptical-shaped lawn (once used as a tennis court) surrounded by borders of rare trees and shrubs, including several fine specimens of Chilean myrtle *Luma apiculata*.

Botanist, landscape designer and gardening author John Claudius Louden visited Dunster in 1842, and described plants on the terraces like lemons, Mediterranean pomegranates, myrtles, passion flowers and wisteria. Today the National Trust continues to exploit the warmth and shelter of these south-facing terraces and has brought together a wonderful collection of plants from all over the world, including Japanese bananas, Mexican agaves, hot-coloured Central American dahlias, large-leaved Tetrapanax from Taiwan and phormiums from New Zealand. There is also a National Collection of *Arbutus sp.*, and in spring the grounds come alive with thousands of spring-flowering bulbs.

Plant niches on the terrace

❊ EAST LAMBROOK MANOR GARDENS

East Lambrook Manor Gardens are without doubt one of England's best loved and influential gardens of the twentieth century. Created between 1938 and 1969 by renowned plantswoman Margery Fish, it has become an iconic landscape for anyone trying to recreate the quintessential English cottage garden style in their own garden. It was awarded Grade I listing in 1992 and is now famous throughout the world, but in truth much of what Margery did in the early years was by necessity given the lack of manpower and austerity experienced in Britain following the Second World War. It was simply no longer feasible to have the expense of teams of gardeners maintaining gardens in the style of pre-war Hidcote and Sissinghurst. Nevertheless, Margery's ability and talent for combining old-fashioned and contemporary plants, in a relaxed and informal manner, created at East Lambrook Manor not only a grand cottage garden on a domestic scale and something that everyone could relate to, but also a unique and extraordinary place of great beauty and charm.

In essence this is an informal cottage garden of densely planted beds and borders, segmented by small paths interspersed with areas of grass. The whole is managed with a light touch in controlling growth, colour, form and fragrance. ▸

East Lambrook Manor

❀ EAST LAMBROOK MANOR GARDENS

◀ An important part of the work carried out by Margery Fish at East Lambrook was the conservation of rare and endangered species, and still to this day the garden boasts an astonishing collection of plants she saved from extinction. This is without doubt a plantsman's garden and contains many rare snowdrops, along with extensive collections of unusual hellebores and hardy cranesbill geraniums.

Much has been done to restore and revitalise the garden since the Millennium and new owners who arrived at East Lambrook in 2008 have continued this work. Areas of the garden tackled in recent years include The Terraces, White Garden, Hellebore Woodland Garden and Long Border. In the process, several of Margery Fish's rare plants, which were thought to be lost to cultivation, have been rediscovered and saved.

A completely new garden creation is The Scented Garden, which runs along the edge of a seating area where visitors can enjoy the fragrances emitted from plants such as daphnes, roses, honeysuckles and lavenders.

In addition, Margery Fish's Plant Nursery has been relocated to its original 1950s site and continues to specialise in cottage garden plants and interesting perennials, many of which are propagated from plants growing within the garden.

◀ Densely packed borders

Silver Garden and trough

❈ THE EDEN PROJECT

The Eden Project is without doubt one of the most spectacular and inspirational modern-day horticultural creations. It is also much more than just a garden. Dubbed by its founder Sir Tim Smit as 'a theatre of plants', it cleverly tells the story of man's interaction and dependence upon plants.

The journey from the Eden Project's own germination in a disused and flooded china clay pit near St Austell to one of the most iconic British landmark projects of the twenty-first century is a perfect example of triumph over adversity.

Complicated planning issues, uncertainties over funding and dissenters on several fronts, all paled into insignificance in January 1999 when the land set aside for the main visitor centre building slid into the bottom of the pit, to be followed by 43 million gallons of water. Little more than two years later, on 17 March 2001, with vast geodesic biomes gleaming in watery spring sunshine, the Eden Project opened to the public.

Today the world's largest tropical rainforest in captivity is housed within Eden's main biome, which also includes a canopy walkway and a 65-foot-high (20-metre) waterfall to increase humidity. Here you will find a fascinating array of plants from equatorial regions of the world, including Amazonia, West Africa, Malaysia and Oceania. ▶

The Eden Project biomes

Inside the tropical biome ▶

◀ There are additional biomes representing warm temperate zones such as the Mediterranean, California and South Africa, which, although initially slow to establish, have now come of age. Growing outside the biomes are further plant collections from temperate climates found in the British Isles. In total, Eden grows over 135,000 plants, which are representative of approximately 4,500 different species. In 2005 a new education centre called 'The Core' opened and reinforces the message that humanity is dependent on the plant world.

What makes Eden different to so many botanical gardens is that although the messages may stay the same, the way they are delivered is constantly changing, quite often through the use of the arts. Be it sculpture, music, poetry or painting, things are constantly in motion at Eden and there is a vibrancy around the site that is seldom sustained in other gardens. However, do not think for a moment that this is at odds with the aesthetic appreciation of plants; it isn't, there are stunning floral gardens at Eden throughout the year and the standard of plant expertise and maintenance on display is excellent.

Theatre of plants

❀ FORDE ABBEY GARDENS

More than 900 years of history are encapsulated in this delightful former Cistercian monastery (a private home since 1649) and its Grade II listed 30-acre (12-hectare) award-winning gardens.

Although the original monastic gardens are long gone, some of the infrastructure associated with the monastery remains, including the Great Pond, which was originally used to power a grain mill and now provides a reservoir for water features such as Forde's Long Pond. The beginnings of the present garden were laid out by eighteenth-century owner Francis Gwyn. He created lawns, built garden walls, planted many of the ancient yews and limes and used water from the Great Pond to create three further ponds and cascades. Little more was done to the garden until the latter part of the nineteenth century, when the large kitchen garden was created at the back of the abbey and evergreen shrubberies, typical of the Victorian era, were planted to the front.

Over the past 100 years and using the legacy and infrastructure of these earlier garden features, the Roper family, the Forde Abbey owners since 1905, have developed a garden which truly has something for everyone. The front of the house is bordered by colourful bedding, dominated in spring by wallflowers that give way to salvias and heliotropes. ▸

Forde Abbey

❀ FORDE ABBEY GARDENS

◀ Beds beneath the cloisters are planted with daphnes, camellias, chrysanthemums and nerines, while growing against the Chapel wall is a magnificent *Magnolia grandiflora*. The east wall of the house is covered by three varieties of wisteria *Wisteria sinensis*, *Wisteria floribunda* 'Macrobotrys', and the white-flowering *Wisteria brachybotrys* 'Shiro-kapitan'.

Running parallel to the Long Pond is the main herbaceous border. Seen at its best from July onwards, the predominant plantings are delphiniums, aconitums, dahlias and asters, while in sheltered positions beneath the facing wall are tender plants such as the Californian tree anemone *Carpenteria californica* and Chilean *Azara serrata*.

In the early 1900s, a bog garden was created in a silted area of the Great Pond and today displays a large collection of candelabra primulas, meconopsis, iris and other Asiatic moisture-loving plants such as *Lysichitum camtschatcensis*. There is also a superb rock garden full of alpines and an arboretum started by Geoffrey Roper in 1947.

The latest addition to the garden is the Centenary Fountain, opened in 2005 to celebrate the centenary of the Roper family's arrival at Forde, it has a maximum height of 160 feet (49 metres) and is the highest powered water fountain in England.

◀ Forde Abbey in spring

Summer kitchen garden

❀ GLENDURGAN

Glendurgan's garden is positioned in a collection of four verdant valleys, which flow right down to the Helford River. At the higher end of the main valley sits Glendurgan House and the National Trust car park and visitor centre, and at the lower end the delightful hamlet of Durgan, where a cluster of twenty or so white-washed former fishermen's cottages huddle up close to the water's edge. In between the two are 25 acres (10 hectares) of glorious Cornish woodland garden, punctuated by the surprising and altogether more formal feature of a cherry laurel maze. Originally laid out in 1833 by Alfred Fox (brother of Charles Fox who created Trebah Garden), this asymmetrical maze, which has at its centre a thatched gazebo, was completely restored to celebrate the centenary of the National Trust in 1995. Alongside the maze is a delightful pool fringed by astilbes and sheltered by a Himalayan cedar *Cedrus deodara,* while above lies the 'Holy Bank', displaying a collection of plants associated with the Bible.

Perhaps more in keeping with a Cornish woodland garden is the Camellia Walk, originally laid out by Alfred's grandson George over a century ago and extended more recently by the National Trust. ▸

Durgan

Michelia syn. Magnolia doltsopa ▸

◀ Here traditional cultivars such as 'Captain Rawes', 'Cornish Snow', 'Debutante' and 'Ville de Nantes' mix with more modern varieties of *Camellia reticulate*, including 'Butterfly Wings', 'Crimson Rose' and 'Lion's Head'. Not to be outdone, rhododendrons are also here in force – big, billowing specimens with huge domes of flower, sometimes fragrant as with the Loderi hybrids, sometimes vibrantly coloured (as with the electric blue *Rhododendron augustinii*) and sometimes flowering well on into summer, which is the nature of the snow-white flowered 'Polar Bear'. However, any visit to Glendurgan would not be complete without paying homage to the magnificent *Michelia* syn. *Magnolia doltsopa* which is positioned in the central valley. A tender evergreen tree from Yunnan, Tibet and the eastern Himalayas, it produces sweetly fragrant, creamy-white water-lily-like flowers, which emerge from cinnamon-coloured velvet buds in April.

No matter what time of year you visit Glendurgan, the topography, pools and streams will inevitably draw you ever downwards, until the tangy spice of seaweed will begin to fill the air. Soon after, you emerge on Durgan's shoreline to a vista which takes in the Helford and the cove-pocked fringes of the Lizard Peninsula beyond. It is truly a little piece of paradise, supplemented, of course, by a wonderful garden.

Glendurgan Maze

✿ GREAT CHALFIELD MANOR

Great Chalfield Manor is a moated fifteenth-century house with decorative architecture of gables, oriel windows and gargoyles all played out in mellow, honey-coloured walls and dark timbers. It was restored by Robert Fuller under the guidance of architect Sir Harold Brakspear, between 1905 and 1912. Fuller purchased the property from his father and it remains today the home of his grandson Robert Floyd and his family, who continue to manage the property in conjunction with the National Trust, who were given the property by Robert Fuller in 1943.

At the same time as renovating the manor house, Fuller also commissioned artist and Arts and Crafts garden designer Alfred Parsons RA to redesign the garden in a way that would sit comfortably alongside the house, adjacent fourteenth-century parish church and surrounding moat.

Parsons kept a large lawn but introduced terraces, walls, flagged paths, topiary pavilions, lily pool and a fine gazebo. More than a century later, the infrastructure of the garden is as relevant as it ever was, with features such as the four yew topiary pavilions, now giant venerable green sculpted 'houses' beloved by adults and children alike, who gleefully explore their dark green interiors. ▶

The moat at Great Chalfield Manor

✿ GREAT CHALFIELD MANOR

◀ The walls of the manor are clothed in a delightful mix of fragrant pineapple broom *Argyrocytisus battandieri* and yellow Banksian roses *Rosa banksiae* 'Lutea'. Alongside the stone-flagged terraces, several substantial herbaceous borders, recently replanted by the family, are a masterclass in the use of colour, with perhaps the blue border the finest of them all with its intimate mix of hardy geraniums, irises and nepeta. The borders are at their best between June and September.

In late winter snowdrops and aconites brighten the banks of the spring-fed lower moat, to be followed by daffodils, tulips and Queen Anne's lace, all of which overflow into the orchard where apple blossom falls like pale pink snow in May. Throughout the garden there are roses by the score, including several splendid, old-fashioned varieties such as *Rosa* 'Mme. Caroline Testout' and *Rosa* 'Bennett's Seedling' in the courtyard, *Rosa* 'Old Blush China' in the churchyard, *Rosa* 'Rambling Rector' and *Rosa* 'Sanders White rambler' scrambling through the apple trees and *Rosa* 'The Fairy' near the lower moat.

In autumn, sky-blue asters flower below the terrace, complemented by fiery reds and golds of Virginia creeper close to the garden entrance. Both the manor and garden featured in the 2008 film *The Other Boleyn Girl*.

◀ Terrace borders

Yew topiary pavilions

✤ GREENCOMBE

There are some gardens, which, given their location, simply shouldn't work. One such garden is Greencombe. Almost everything about Greencombe's location suggests that it should be a struggle to grow ornamental plants successfully. The garden faces north; light intensity is low; in places the site is very steep; little decent soil exists; it sits high on a cliff facing the winds that funnel up the Bristol Channel; plants and soil are constantly bombarded with salt; no natural water runs through the garden; and for two months of the year the sun does not even manage to make it above the horizon. Despite all of this Greencombe is a truly wonderful garden, full of interesting and beautiful plants and a real plantsman's garden to boot, actually plantswoman's, as this is the garden and creation of Joan Lorraine.

To be strictly accurate it is the creation of Horace Stroud, who came to Greencombe in 1946; Joan arrived in 1966 and by then Mr Stroud had made three terraces, levelled and shaped the main lawn, built a moon gate in the garden wall, acquired woodland to the west of the house and planted within it 1,000 rhododendron and azalea cuttings gleaned from Cornish gardens. However, what Joan Lorraine has added to Greencombe over the past fifty years has taken it from being a pleasant garden to a great garden. ▸

Tree fern in the Woodland Garden

Hydrangeas on the lawn ▸

◀ You will find an inspirational mix of trees, shrubs, climbers, bulbs, herbaceous plants and ferns. The beds around the formal lawns are immaculately maintained and support a tapestry of alstroemeria, callistemon, roses, lilies, hydrangeas, maples and camellias. Garden walls are bedecked in unusual climbers and wall-shrubs, such as the white-flowering form of the 'parrot's bill' *Clianthus puniceus* 'Albus' and *Schisandra chinensis*. By contrast the woodland areas, which are traversed by narrow pathways that follow the contours of the slope, are full of choice species – rhododendrons, azaleas, myrtles, eucryphias, hellebores and trilliums. Here too are National Collections of erythronium, gaultheria, polystichum and vaccinium.

No sprays or chemicals are used in this garden; it is completely organic and has been for almost fifty years, which makes the excellent health and vigour of the planting even more astonishing. All of which goes to show that no matter what the problems are in your own garden you should be able to create something really special – or perhaps Joan Lorraine is actually Pomona (the Roman goddess of gardens) in disguise!

Clianthus puniceus

❀ HARDY'S COTTAGE

It faces west, and around the back and sides
High beeches, bending, hang a veil of boughs,
And sweep against the roof. Wild honeysucks
Climb on the wall, and seem to sprout a wish
(If we may fancy wish of trees and plants)
To overtop the apple-trees hard by.
Red roses, lilacs, variegated box
Are there in plenty, and such hardy flowers
As flourish best untrained.

Extract from 'Domicilium' – Thomas Hardy

The thatched cottage at Higher Bockhampton, near Dorchester, where Thomas Hardy was born in 1840 and lived until the age of thirty-four, has changed little over the past 175 years. It is still relatively secluded (despite the recent introduction by the National Trust of a nearby visitor centre) and it is still possible in your mind's eye to see Hardy, head bowed over his small wooden desk writing his earlier novels, which include *Under the Greenwood Tree* and *Far from the Madding Crowd*. Alongside the cottage is Thorncombe Woods, an ancient, semi-natural woodland, which was the inspiration for several of ▶

The setting of 'Domicilium'

❋ HARDY'S COTTAGE

◀ the sylvan scenes that appear within his works. Behind the cottage still lays the remains of 'heath and furze', the beginning of Egdon Heath, which blasted landscape so prominent in *The Return of the Native*.

We are not exactly sure when Hardy wrote his poem 'Domicilium' (it was most probably sometime between 1856 and 1862), but the descriptions of the garden within the poem add justification to the way the National Trust maintain and manage the garden today. Without the poem it would be easy to say that the Trust has simply recreated an idealised chocolate box image of what a nineteenth-century English country cottage garden should have looked like, complete with roses and honeysuckles around the door. With the poem we can see exactly what Hardy saw, and as such the Trust has been faithful to that vision. Informal untrained plantings of lilacs, foxgloves, lupins, aquilegias, peonies, primroses and pinks are allowed to overflow on to winding gravel paths, local old varieties of apple grow in the orchard and the fruit and vegetable patch is full of 'herbs and esculents', including currants, gooseberries and old-fashioned varieties of 'Portland Black' potatoes. This atmospheric, historical garden is probably as near to time travel that any of us will ever get, and some would say to heaven too.

◀ Plants overflow onto winding gravel paths

Cottage garden

❀ HESTERCOMBE

Widely known for its Lutyens and Jekyll Edwardian garden, Hestercombe is in fact a unique combination of three different periods of English garden history.

The earliest is the 35-acre (14-hectare) Grade I listed Georgian landscape, laid out to the north of the house in a long, narrow wooded combe (Hester Combe), by Coplestone Warre Bamfylde between 1750 and 1786. His plan – perfectly executed – was for an Arcadian landscape with circular walks, which passed a series of reveals, vistas, statuary, lakes and architecture. Other than the felling of timber in the 1960s, this landscape had changed little since its creation, and over the past fifteen years has been carefully restored to its former glory. It includes several fine examples of garden architecture from the period such as the Doric Temple, Mausoleum and Gothic Alcove, where stunning views are revealed across the Vale of Taunton to the Blackdown Hills beyond. The centrepiece of the garden is the Great Cascade, a theatrical masterpiece with white water tumbling down a series of falls to a lawn bespotted with carefully placed boulders.

In 1873, Hestercombe was acquired by the 1st Viscount Portman, who undertook considerable remodelling of the house and created the Victorian Terrace to the south of the house. ▶

Jekyll and Lutyen's Great Plat Garden

Great Cascade ▶

❋ HESTERCOMBE

◀ Now restored, the Terrace has at its heart a series of beds planted, in typical Victorian fashion, with seasonally changing exuberant and colourful bedding schemes. Portman also created a shrubbery typical of the period from the late 1870s and 1880s. In this design he was undoubtedly influenced by William Robinson's book *The Wild Garden*, first published in 1870. Restoration of the Victorian shrubbery in the style of Robinson began in 1899, and today it is one of very few examples from this period in garden history.

In 1904 the Hon. Edward Portman commissioned Sir Edwin Lutyens to create a new formal garden. Lutyens' designs for the garden, which included orangery, pergola, terraces, rill, walls, steps, pools, paving and seating are widely acclaimed as Lutyens at his best, as are the planting schemes designed by Gertrude Jekyll. Using borders of graduated colour and planting in drifts, she complemented perfectly the hard landscaping of Lutyens. Originally established over four years from 1904 until 1908, Hestercombe's Formal Garden is considered to be the finest example of the collaborative work undertaken by this inspirational and influential partnership. Once abandoned and now faithfully restored, it is today a garden of tranquillity and great beauty.

Rose pergola

❁ KILLERTON

This large hillside garden, situated high above the flood plain of the River Exe, is surrounded by woodland, parkland (with sheep grazing beneath ancient sweet chestnut trees) and farmland. In all, the estate extends to over 6,000 acres (2,428 hectares). The garden was originally laid out in the 1770s by head gardener John Veitch for owner Sir Thomas Dyke Acland, and was designed in the landscape parkland style of the day; however it did not stay that way for long. By the early 1800s, Acland had helped Veitch set up a plant nursery at nearby Budlake. This was the start of the most influential nursery company of the nineteenth century and soon John Veitch's son, James, from their larger nursery site in Exeter, was commissioning plant hunters to scour the British Empire and beyond in search of new botanical discoveries. As each new plant introduction was made, the close relationship between Veitch and Acland meant that Killerton received first pick and so the grounds filled up with plant rarities never before grown in Britain. For over a century this connection was maintained, the results of which can be seen today in the arboretum, which climbs a volcanic outcrop known as Killerton Clump to the north of the house. Here, thrusting forth mighty conical-shaped crowns that punctuate the skyline, are original introductions of giant redwood *Sequoiadendron giganteum*, collected as seed in California by William Lobb in 1853. ▶

Main lawn with Woodland Garden

◀ On the lower slopes and within island beds on the main lawn are close to 100 different species of rhododendron, some over 200 years old and originally introduced from Japan and China.

In the early twentieth century, the famous Victorian gardening writer William Robinson advised on the garden and as a result the Great Terrace to the west of the salmon-pink walled house was created. Originally planted with roses, it now houses an attractive collection of low-growing, flowering shrubs – many of Mediterranean origin.

Running away at a right-angle to the house are a series of herbaceous borders planted in a way that bring colour and interest to the garden from spring right through until the dew-days of early October. Beyond the lawns a delightful thatched summer house can be found. Built for Lady Lydia Acland in 1808, it later became known as the Bear's Hut after their grandson Gilbert housed a Canadian black bear here. Close by is the ice house and a steep-sided rock garden through which a small stream descends via a series of pools.

◀ Rhododendron and white abulition

Woodland Garden

❈ KILVER COURT

Between the fifteenth and the nineteenth century, Kilver Court, located in the Somerset market town of Shepton Mallet, flourished as the location for eleven woollen mills. Power for the mills came from the River Sheppey that ran through the grounds and its flow was controlled by a series of mill ponds, dams and weirs.

In the 1850s, the Somerset and Dorset Railway built a magnificent 317-yard (290-metre), twenty-seven-arched viaduct directly behind the mills. Around this time, Kilver Court was purchased by Ernest Jardine MP, who turned the mills into a 'model factory' producing silk and lace. For the well-being of his factory employees he created a landscaped garden called Jardine's Park and turned the mill ponds into boating lakes, formed paths that meandered through attractive plantings and grew fruit and vegetables to provide healthy meals for his employees.

In the late 1950s the site was bought by the Showering family, famous for producing Babycham. Francis Showering, an enthusiastic and knowledgeable gardener, created a new garden on site based on a 1963 Chelsea Flower Show gold medal-winning rock garden. Working on a much larger-scale to the original, because of the gigantic proportions of the adjacent viaduct, the garden became a bold and modern design statement. For more than thirty years it was beautifully maintained but seldom opened to the public. ▸

Kilver Court pond and viaduct

Box parterre at Kilver Court ▸

◂ In 1995, Roger Saul (founder of the fashion and home designer label Mulberry), on the lookout for new headquarters for the company, stumbled across the site. 'I knew I was looking for something which was modern but also had style', he remarked. Once he had viewed the property, Roger was confident this was the place.

With Mulberry installed in the mills and plans afoot to turn the neighbouring old schoolhouse into a Mulberry factory shop, Roger turned his attention to the garden. Replacing original specimens that had outgrown their position, he then turned what he considered to be the garden's least inspiring feature – 'a distinctly "municipal parks department planting" of corporation roses' into a French-inspired box parterre, in-filled with lavender, santolina and iris and flanked by two large herbaceous borders each ending with evergreen *Magnolia grandiflora*, creating a vista to the rock garden and viaduct beyond.

In 2008 Kilver Court's garden opened to the public and today this beautiful man-made landscape, with its fascinating history stretching back over 500 years, is visited by thousands who combine a visit to the garden with some very chic retail therapy.

Rock and Water Garden

❉ KINGSTON LACY

This Grade II listed, 32-acre (13-hectare) garden near Wimborne in Dorset is administered by the National Trust in a way that manages to capture the very essence of Edwardian England. This is not to say that the whole garden was created during that era (far from it), but it oozes the attention to detail and the standard of maintenance and horticultural excellence that would have been commonplace in the confident, self-assured British Empire years of the early twentieth century.

From the seventeenth to the twentieth century, Kingston Lacy was the seat of the Bankes family. The original landscape they created was one of a formal garden with trees, including a fine avenue of lime trees that still exists today and lead to Nursery Wood, where, at a much later date, an extensive collection of camellias, rhododendrons, azaleas and flowering cherries was planted.

Much of the garden on view today owes its beginnings to the vision of Henrietta Bankes (1867–1953). A remarkable lady in many ways, she turned a large proportion of Kingston Lacy into a hospital for returning injured soldiers during the First World War. However, her most tangible legacy probably lies within the garden. ▶

Sunken Garden and House

◀ The Italian Terrace displays urns, vases, lions in bronze and marble, marble containers for bay trees and an Egyptian obelisk and sarcophagus. The Sunk Garden and Parterre were laid out by Henrietta in 1899, in memory of her husband, and still today remains true to the early twentieth-century seasonal planting schemes she designed. One of her greatest achievements was the recently restored Japanese Garden. Covering 7.5 acres (3 hectares) in the southern woodland shelter belt, it was laid out by Henrietta around 1910 and is one of the largest of its kind in England. At its heart is a formal tea garden complete with granite lanterns, bamboos, a dry stone stream, teahouse and a waiting arbour. There is also a maple glade, quarry garden, evergreen garden and cherry garden.

In the shade of mature yew trees, Kingston Lacy also boasts a Fernery – again the inspiration of Henrietta Bankes – which displays forty different varieties of ferns as well as housing the National Collection (Plant Heritage) of *Anemone nemorosa*.

The latest restoration project has been the Victorian Kitchen Garden, which grows, as it did a century ago, a comprehensive range of fruit, vegetables and cut flowers. There are several restored Victorian glasshouses, one of which houses a fine collection of orchids.

◀ Japanese Garden Pond
(*Courtesy of Elliot Brown, Flickr*)

Kingston Lacy Garden

✤ KINGSTON MAURWARD GARDENS

Set in undulating Dorset countryside, Kingston Maurward spans three distinct periods in garden history. The first period relates to the original landscaped park of some 35 acres (14 hectares), which combines wide grassy swathes with long vistas to a lake carefully framed by individual trees and blocks of woodland. The fine Georgian mansion the garden surrounds was built in 1720, and the park laid out soon after. The garden is in the style of what became known as the 'Jardin Anglais' (English Garden Style), a form much popularised by Lancelot 'Capability' Brown.

The second period of garden creation took place immediately following the First World War, when Kingston Maurward owners, the Hanbury family, created a series of formal gardens to the west of the mansion. Perhaps better known for their garden at La Mortola on the Italian Riviera, their handiwork in Dorset is just as impressive and involved them using stone-flagged terracing, balustrading, stone steps and close-clipped yew and box hedging to border exquisite intimate spaces which run off on different axes. The north/south axis takes in the Italian Renaissance-style Red Garden, Mediterranean Border and Double Herbaceous Border. The east–west axis leads from the Brick Garden, to the Terrace Border and the south front of the mansion. ▸

Terrace steps to the garden

Kingston Maurward Georgian mansion ▸

(Image courtesy of Julie Poad)

◀ Each of these spaces has a central feature or focal point, such as a pool, statue, maze or theme, like the Rose Garden or Penstemon Terrace, and as such has a distinct character. It is very Edwardian in its concept, but all in all is wonderful in its use of plants, form and colour and provides endless ideas for use back home.

The third phase in this remarkable garden's history relates to its recent use as a training ground for students, who have, since 1990, attended Kingston Maurward College while studying land-based educational courses, including horticulture. As a result, the students and staff have restored the Hanbury gardens to their former glory and added several new features along the way.

A charming Japanese-style garden lies adjacent to the north shore of the lake. It is an intimate and harmonious space containing both upright pillar and broader snow lanterns and a *Tsububai* (a stone hand-washing basin used before taking part in a tea ceremony). Planting is simple but effective and includes dwarf bamboos, evergreen Kurume azaleas and several cultivars of Japanese maple *Acer palmatum,* all overlooked by two Chusan palms *Trachycarpus fortunei*, each more than a century old.

Subtropical terrace planting

❋ KNIGHTSHAYES

Considered for many years one of the foremost National Trust gardens in Britain, Knightshayes has gone through difficult times recently. Storms and disease have devastated both the protective belts of conifers outside the garden and the over-storey of mature larch trees within. Consequently, many smaller choice and tender plants have struggled due to increased exposure to wind and lower temperatures. Hopefully the worst is now behind the garden, and new planting and maintenance regimes will ensure this important plant collection survives and indeed thrives in the forthcoming decades.

Notwithstanding the difficulties, Knightshayes is still an excellent garden and one worth visiting at any time of year. Both the Court and garden are positioned high on the eastern edge of the Exe Valley with far-reaching views over rolling Devon countryside to Tiverton. The property is approached along a rising drive through Victorian parkland studded with mature oak, beech, cedar and pine.

To the rear of the Court is a stable block (now visitor catering and retail units) and a 2-acre (0.8-hectare) restored Victorian walled kitchen garden (restored in 2002), complete with corner turrets, tiered beds and central pool. ▸

Garden rooms

◀ The top south-facing wall is bordered with tender and exotic ornamental shrubs and climbers; however, the majority of the garden is given over to cultivating heritage varieties of fruit and vegetables. Overall it is a splendid example of a productive Victorian country house garden.

The bones of the present-day ornamental garden are contemporary; the building of the house was by William Burgess between 1869 and 1874. The terraces in front of the house were set out by Edward Kemp during this period, although the current planting is restrained compared to the original Victorian bedding schemes. Battlement-crested hedging defines a series of garden rooms comprising paved courtyards, Mediterranean-style plantings of cistus, lavender, rosemary, agapanthus and other silver-foliaged and sun-loving plants, standard willow-leaved pears *Pyrus salicifolia* 'Pendula', terraces of alpines, troughs, statuary, manicured lawns and topiary hounds chasing a topiary fox.

Set apart from the house is 'The Garden in the Wood'. Created in 1950 by Sir John and Lady Amory, this remarkable 25-acre (10-hectare) garden comprised of meandering walks and glades, supports a fascinating collection of rare ornamental plants ranging from pulmonarias, omphalodes, hellebores and erythroniums, through geraniums, ferns and euphorbias, to tender rhododendrons, magnolias and camellias that you would normally associate with milder Cornish gardens further west. This garden is a must for anyone with a serious interest in plants.

◀ *Magnolia campbellii* in The Garden in the Wood

Autumn at Knightshayes

❈ KNOLL GARDENS

The story of Knoll Gardens goes back to the early 1970s, when John and Enid May began to turn an old carrot field and adjacent scrub woodland into an ornamental and diverse garden of plants ranging from rhododendrons to phygelius. Before too long they had amassed an astonishing collection and the garden became known as Wimborne Botanic Garden. In 1988 they sold the garden, and in 1994 it came into the care of Neil Lucas among others. Twenty years on Neil is now sole owner of Knoll Gardens and a leading authority on ornamental grasses to boot, having written several books on the subject and appeared many times on TV.

The garden today is laid out in an informal naturalistic way, with unusual trees and shrubs, many planted by the Mays back in the 1970s, including some stunning eucalyptus, providing a superb backdrop to thousands of grasses and flowering perennials grown in island beds and borders. Knoll is home to one of the UK's most extensive collections of grasses and as such provides a living text book on how best to grow them. Throughout the garden they are planted to beautiful effect and demonstrate a new route to an affordable, low-maintenance, wildlife friendly, sustainable garden. ▶

Knoll, a garden of ornametal grasses
(*Images courtesy of Peter Curbishley, Flickr*)

Ornamental trees provide ▶
a backdrop to the grasses

Although Knoll is only a little over 4 acres (1.6 hectares) in size, the many different areas, winding pathways and constantly changing views give an impression of a much larger garden. There is a relaxed and intimate atmosphere here and the mature trees throughout the garden add a sense of seclusion, heightened in the summer months when some of the grasses may grow in excess of 6 feet (2 metres) tall.

In some ways the garden could be considered to be at its best in the autumn, when the seed heads on many of the grasses reach perfection and the autumn leaves burst into flame on the trees and shrubs, however Knoll is truly a garden for all seasons. Alongside the grasses there is a large and ever increasing range of flowering perennials and native plants. Each year sees new plantings and themes as the garden evolves, and Neil explores new ways of growing and combining plants for maximum effect. Recent plantings include tender exotics and drought tolerant plants in the newly extended Mediterranean-style gravel garden. There are also areas which grow plants suitable for damp soils. National Collections (Plant Heritage formerly NCCPG) of deciduous ceanothus, phygelius and pennisetums are also held here.

Wisteria-clad pergola
(*Image courtesy of Peter Curbishley, Flickr*)

❁ LAMORRAN

Lamorran hugs the cliff face high above St Mawes on the Roseland Peninsula in a way that is reminiscent of the gardens of La Mortella on the Italian island of Ischia. From the garden there are superb views across the bay to St Anthony's Headland and lighthouse.

Facing due south and sloping towards the sea, garden temperatures remain above freezing throughout most winters. The result is that owner Robert Dudley-Cooke and his head gardener of twenty-three years, Mark Brent, are able to grow a range of tender, subtropical plants seldom seen in other British gardens, including thirty-five different species of palm. Jelly Palm *Butia capitata* from South America and the Canary Island Date Palm *Phoenix canariensis* not only thrive here but self-seed themselves around the garden!

Robert and his Italian wife Maria moved to Lamorran from Surrey thirty-three years ago. Back then the garden was little more than a steep slope falling away towards St Mawes. Robert's idea was to create an informal, romantic terraced garden with curving gravel paths and occasional 'reveals' of the sea.

Today Lamorran is everything he hoped for and much more. A series of terraces, each with a different theme, begin close to the house, with the formal top terrace containing a koi carp pool and a walled garden full of terracotta, olives and fragrant jasmine. ▶

Summer house view to the sea

◀ From here rhododendron and Japanese maple-shaded paths follow streams, cascades and pools, fringed by evergreen Hinomayo azaleas, ferns and bamboos, before arriving at a Cupola, an attractive domed metal structure supported by pillars of stone with sublime views across the sea. Here tree ferns abound, but not just *Dicksonia Antarctica*, the hardy Tasmanian tree fern; there are over ten different species, including the beautiful black-stemmed *Cyathea medullaris* and the rare *Cyathea tomentosissima*, which is endemic to Papua New Guinea.

On the next terrace down shade is minimal, and below a summer house Mediterranean banks of sage-green succulents, including agaves, aloes and puyas, add contrast and structure to swathes of flowering cistus and bright orange gazanias, while blue-spiked echiums stand to attention overhead. Elsewhere, the stonework of Grecian Arcadian follies and ruins provides further vistas to the maritime seascapes beyond and, if that were not enough, Cleopatra's Pool, bedecked by feathery papyrus, transports the visitor to yet another ancient civilisation.

Lamorran is a landscape like no other and one that most definitely deserves its place as one of Cornwall's great gardens.

◀ Arcadian view to St Anthony's Headland

Cleopatra's Pool

❀ LANHYDROCK

Ancient oaks, beech and avenues of sycamore planted in 1635 line the rolling parkland approach to Lanhydrock, and the first glimpse of St Hydroc's grey-turreted church tower, surrounded by copper beech and billowing canopies of rhododendron, is sublimely beautiful.

Soon the lichen-encrusted slate roof of the house, which is arranged on three sides of a central courtyard, can be seen nestling deep into the wooded hillside, which rises almost 200 feet (61 metres) immediately behind.

The present house (other than the entrance porch and the north wing) is little more than 130 years old, the original seventeenth-century property having been severely damaged by fire in 1881. It was given to the National Trust by the 7th Viscount Clifden in 1953. The formal gardens outside, which are set within the confines of Lanhydrock's castellated walls, feature immaculate lawns with twenty-nine clipped topiary Irish yew cones *Taxus baccata* var. *Fastigiata*; bronze urns from the Chateau de Bagatelle in Paris; rose beds; Victorian box-edged parterre planted with spring bulbs followed by summer bedding; and herbaceous circular beds themed for spring and autumn interest.

The way to the 30-acre (12-hectare) upper garden is through wrought-iron gates just above the parterre. ▸

Lanhydrock House

Borlase's Stream ▸

◀ Originally Victorian shrubberies, the 7th Lord Clifden replanted the slopes with exotic ornamental trees and shrubs from the 1930s onwards. Today, high above the roof of the house, it is to the Veitchii Border where large magnolia blooms hang low over the churchyard wall that the spring visitor should head. Here the air is heady with fragrance from choice shrubs such as *Corylopsis glabrescens* and *Osmanthus burkwoodii,* complemented by *Daphne bholua* 'Jacqueline Postill'. By early summer the fragrances have changed to mock orange and rose and spectacular cream-coloured flowering bracts of Chinese dogwoods *Cornus kousa* hold centre stage. A final kaleidoscope of colour comes from autumnal foliage of Japanese maples, Persian ironwoods and spindles.

Throughout the year Borlase's Stream, a fast flowing runnel named after one-time head gardener Peter Borlase, springs out from the hillside into a dipping well virtually hidden by Royal Fern *Osmunda regalis.* Its passage through the garden is clearly evident from waterside plantings of astilbes, arum lilies, rodgersias and candelabra primulas. Close by an old thatched gardener's cottage, last formerly occupied in 1885 has *Camellia reticulata* 'Captain Rawes' growing over its walls. Paths criss-cross the hillside in an ever-climbing fashion until by a cob summerhouse views open out to Caradon Hill and Bodmin Moor.

Woodland Garden

❋ LOST GARDENS OF HELIGAN

In the nineteenth and early twentieth centuries, Heligan was typical of many country estates of that time. Owned by the Tremayne family for 400 years, it comprised a main house, ancillary buildings, barns, stables, mill and estate workers cottages. The land, around 1,000 acres in total (400 hectares), included formal, ornamental and productive gardens with parkland grazing beyond. The estate was self-sufficient in most of its needs, including fruit, vegetables and flowers. The First World War changed all of that. Across Britain men left country estates to fight for 'King and Country', millions did not return, and by 1919 the country's coffers were exhausted by the war effort.

Lack of manpower, money and a wish by the working classes for something better than before, meant that the country estate way of life, which had changed little in centuries, was in decline. At Heligan much of the estate and the gardens fell into disrepair. That is until 16 February 1990, when Tim Smit entered the garden, initially in search of a site to establish a rare animal breed farm and then realising Heligan's potential for a garden restoration ... the rest, as they say, is history.

Today Heligan offers the chance to see 200 acres (80 hectares) of superbly restored estate gardens that effectively and accurately turn the clock back 100 years. ▸

Italian Garden

✤ LOST GARDENS OF HELIGAN

◀ To the north of the main house are the restored productive gardens. Here you will find glasshouses for grapes, peaches, bananas and melons, also pineapple pits that are once again producing pineapples just as they would have done during the reign of Queen Victoria. In the vegetable garden uniform rows of celeriac, chard, Jerusalem artichokes, globe artichokes, cabbage, asparagus and old varieties of potato all thrive beneath liberal applications of seaweed collected from the nearby Cornish coast. A soft fruit garden, Cornish apple orchard, cut flower garden, tool and potting sheds are also here to be explored.

This is, however, only half of the story, for there is also the restored Victorian pleasure grounds where massive 'Cornish Red' rhododendrons and tender shrubs such as *Cornus capitata*, the Himalayan flowering dogwood, abound. The Italian Garden, 'New Zealand' and Flora's Green all add to the story. Last but not least is The Jungle and Lost Valley, a subtropical paradise full of ferns, foliage and large leaved exotics all accessed by a series of boardwalks. Heligan is a demonstration of horticultural archaeology at its very best.

◀ Kitchen Garden

Peach glasshouses

✤ MAPPERTON

The art of a good garden is that it does not give itself away lightly – all is not immediately revealed on entry – instead a drip feed of surprises ensures enjoyment and interest is maintained throughout. One of the best exponents of this is the Grade II listed garden at Mapperton in Dorset, set in a secret, atmospheric landscaped valley where topography is key.

The garden is designed on three levels, with the top level wrapped around the fine Jacobean manor house. Here a courtyard garden, bedecked in old-fashioned roses and clematis, leads on to a croquet lawn. From here there are fine vistas across hills grazed by sheep and cattle and shaded by ancient trees, but little sign of the rest of the garden; in fact one could be forgiven for thinking 'well, is that all?' However, walk to the edge of the lawn and very much like at Upton House in the north Cotswolds, the land falls away steeply to the Italianate Fountain Court with its sculptured topiary, fountains, canals, statuary and grottoes. It is garden theatre at its finest.

Much of the infrastructure for the garden seen at Mapperton today was created in the 1920s by owner Ethel Labouchere. She, along with architect Charles Pike, designed the garden in memory of her husband Henry, who had perished in the First World War. ▸

Fountain Court Garden

Pond at Mapperton ▸
(*Image courtesy of Peter, Flickr*)

◄ Ethel was an admirer of the work of Harold Peto and there are features here which are reminiscent of Peto's garden at Iford Manor near Bath.

Pools of water, carved stone steps, a pergola and borders brimming with Mediterranean plantings, including several varieties of salvia, lay opposite a neo-classical orangery, built in 1986 by Victor Montagu the father of the present owner. It was Montagu who restored Ethel Labouchere's original design to its former glory and expanded the garden to 15 acres (6 hectares) by developing a wild garden and arboretum in the valley bottom alongside seventeenth-century fishponds.

Today, his son John and wife Carolyn, the Earl and Countess of Sandwich, both knowledgeable gardeners, continue the work with enthusiasm. Around the house they have planted several varieties of evergreen *Magnolia grandiflora* including 'Maryland' and 'Exmouth', established more yew hedging to further enhance the surprise factor of Mrs Labouchere's garden, developed imaginative new planting schemes for the borders and planted the Orangery with citrus and pale pink begonias. This is a garden of the past but definitely one of the future too.

Magnolia grandiflora

❀ MARWOOD HILL

Situated a few miles inland from the North Devon coastal town of Ilfracombe is one of the loveliest gardens in the West Country – Marwood Hill.

The garden was created by Dr Jimmy Smart VMH, who moved to Marwood in 1949. Back then the 8-acre (3.2-hectare) holding consisted of a derelict walled garden, a few old fruit trees, some elms and rough pastureland, all set within a long, steep-sided valley through which a small stream flowed. Dr Smart realised the garden needed structure, and in particular ornamental trees and shrubs, especially camellias and magnolias. By the 1960s he had addressed this to such an extent that he had run out of space and needed to acquire more land! Further rough pastureland on the far side of the valley was duly purchased and planted with a mixture of birch, eucalyptus, eucryphia and maple.

In 1968 the stream was dammed to form two lakes and the surrounding damp soil planted with a wide variety of moisture-loving plants, including primulas, astilbes, iris and hemerocallis. An island in the larger lake was adorned with a beautiful sculpture of a mother and child by the Australian sculptor John Robinson. Shortly afterwards a large greenhouse was erected in the walled garden and filled with tender camellias.

In 1972 Dr Smart invited Malcolm Pharoah to become his head gardener. ▶

View to the lakes

◀ Malcolm had previously worked at the RHS garden at Wisley and brought plenty of new experiences and ideas with him to Marwood. A third lake was added in 1982 followed by a folly and scented arbour in 1986. Since then the stream garden has been extended and plantings of grasses and perennials have added a further dimension to this remarkable garden.

Dr Smart died in 2002, but his garden, which now extends to 20 acres (8 hectares) lives on as a fitting memorial to a truly remarkable man. Today, there are over 800 different cultivars of camellia, close on 100 magnolias and innumerable rhododendrons and cherries. Not only that, this garden also holds National Collections of astilbe, tulbaghia and Japanese iris, which extend the flowering season into late summer.

Unsurprisingly, Marwood has become a popular destination for garden visits and every year thousands of people come in search of 'Dr Smart's garden' and yet it never feels overly busy. Somehow this sheltered valley, with its cascading stream, peaceful lakes and wonderful collection of plants, manages to retain a sense of peace and tranquillity.

◀ Astilbes complement the mother and child sculpture

Valley Gardens

✤ MINTERNE GARDENS

Home of the Churchill and Digby families since 1620, Minterne is a grand house set within a magnificent Grade II listed landscaped valley, originally laid out in the manner of Lancelot 'Capability' Brown's English parkland style in the eighteenth century. It includes a chain of small lakes, streams and cascades, all strategically positioned to provide focal points in a wider landscape of parkland and woodland.

The gardens, which extend to 20 acres (8 hectares), are laid out in a mile-long horseshoe below the house and are renowned for their magnificent collection of flowering shrubs and in particular rhododendrons, including specimens of the giant Himalayan *Rhododendron arboreum* which were planted in the 1850s. Three generations of the Digby family have built up the rhododendron collection, which is founded upon their sponsorship of plant hunting expeditions by pioneering collectors such as Joseph Hooker in the Victorian era, George Forrest, Ernest Wilson and Joseph Rock in the early years of the twentieth century and Frank Kingdon Ward in the 1920s. The present Hon. Henry Digby is continuing in the tradition and along with his head gardener, Ray Abraham, is conserving many of the original introductions and propagating new varieties. ▶

Minterne Bridge with bluebells

Rhododendron arboreum ▶

◀ In spring, to walk alongside Minterne's fast flowing stream surrounded by steep-sided banks and gullies overflowing with rhododendrons is a magical experience that few other gardens can replicate.

At times you could be forgiven for believing you were in Sikkim and literally following in Forrest's footsteps. There are too many species to mention in entirety, but the flavour can be gained by mentioning just two – *Rhododendron hippophaeoides* with funnel-shaped lilac-pink flowers collected by George Forrest in 1913 and *Rhododendron falconeri* with its magnificent waxy creamy-yellow, purple-blotched flowers collected by Joseph Hooker in 1850. It is worth visiting Minterne just to see these two beauties alone, but of course there is much more to this garden.

In spring, *Enkianthus campanulatus* and several fine specimens of the pocket-handkerchief tree *Davidia involucrata* are joined by swathes of wild garlic and bluebells. In summer, South American fragrant-flowering eucryphias and mophead and lacecap hydrangeas take centre stage and in autumn a kaleidoscope of colour from Minterne's fine collection of Japanese maples make an October visit a must. All in all, this is a restful, attractive and botanically important garden, where handwritten plant labels add to the feeling that you are never far away from the great pioneering plant collectors of the nineteenth and early twentieth centuries.

Streamside garden overflowing with plants

❋ MONTACUTE HOUSE

The framework of this beautiful Grade I listed Elizabethan garden, set around an Elizabethan mansion built of mellow golden ham stone, is in essence a rare surviving example of Elizabethan garden design, if somewhat changed from when it was first established in the early 1600s. By 1667, several additional walled gardens and courts had been added, along with a series of orchards and, in the nineteenth century, Ellen Helyar, having married into the owning Phelips family, remodelled much of the internal design with the help of her gardener Mr Pridham, to create her Victorian ideal of an Elizabethan garden.

Today the garden is a triumph of Elizabethan formality that has been gracefully weathered and changed by the intervening centuries, but somehow managed to retain the character and integrity of its youthful self. Decorative, lichen-encrusted architecture abounds with pinnacled balustrades, pavilions, an arcaded garden house and ornate leaded windows contrasting perfectly with sweeping parkland, golden in early summer with swathes of buttercups, and sombre lines of evergreens, such as ninety-six clipped Irish yews which march like an approaching army down the avenues leading to the house. In total there are 260 acres (106 hectares) of parkland and 10 acres (4 hectares) of formally laid out gardens at Montacute. ▶

Montacute House

❈ MONTACUTE HOUSE

◀ The surrealism of the topiary and in particular the giant yew hedge, owes its contours to a freak and heavy snowfall in the winter of 1947, the weight of which bent and twisted the branches so forcefully that they have never re-grown to their original lines. Now clipped to their 'wibbly-wobbly' shape, they are part of an annual mile-long hedge trimming programme at Montacute that takes up to three months to complete.

Recently restored, The Orangery, with its fern-covered cascade of stone and tufa, is once again flowing with water, and in summer the box-edged gravel courtyard nearby is decorated with citrus plants grown in large terracotta pots.

In the sunken flower parterre the beds surrounding the Jacobean-style central fountain are planted with old-fashioned fragrant roses, such as *Rosa moschata* 'Autumnalis'. However, most of the colour and flower at Montacute is reserved for the borders of the East Court, which in places backs onto the ornate balustrade that rises above. Originally designed by Phyllis Reiss from nearby Tintinhull, they are today full of vibrant-coloured herbaceous plants including peonies, *Crambe cordifolia*, *Acanthus mollis* and *Macleaya microcarpa* 'Kelway's Coral Plume', interspersed with purple-leaved shrubs such as *Cotinus* 'Grace' and *Berberis thunbergii* 'Rose Glow'.

◀ Terrace and East Court

Wibbly-wobbly hedge

❈ OVERBECK'S

There are few gardens in Britain where the growing of palms, bananas, citrus and olives is considered as normal as growing geraniums, but that is certainly the case in this 7-acre (2.75-hectare) exotic Mediterranean-like garden at Overbeck's, positioned high on a rocky shelf above the Salcombe estuary. The mild maritime climate here enables an astonishing array of tender subtropical plants to thrive, including a fine specimen of the tropical Asian camphor tree *Cinnamomum camphora*.

The garden surrounds an Edwardian-style villa built in 1913, which now houses a museum. It was home to scientist, inventor and advocate of electrotherapy Otto Overbeck from 1928 until his death in 1937,

when the property was bequeathed to the National Trust. Already established when Overbeck arrived in 1928, the garden, which is a mixture of terraces, banks and small compartments, owes its beginnings to previous owners Mr and Mrs Vereker, however Overbeck built on their work with zealous enthusiasm, planting many tender and unusual plants in this exceptional microclimate. During their stewardship the National Trust has continued to expand and develop the collection.

In 1933 Overbeck wrote to a friend: 'It is so warm and beautiful here. I grow bananas, oranges and pomegranates in the open garden and have 3,000 palm trees planted out in my woods and garden.' ▸

Hot coloured borders at Overbeck's

First Flight by Albert Bruce Joy ▸

◀ Today the garden is in truth a little piece of paradise subdivided into a series of themed garden areas. These include the Statue Garden, a formal area of beds and borders full of high season colour and the delightful bronze statue *First Flight* by Albert Bruce Joy; the Banana Garden, a sub-tropical jungle where bananas and other large-leaved foliage plants grow, including *Hedychium sp.* ginger lilies; the Palm Garden where southern hemisphere South African and Australasian plants flourish beneath a canopy of palms, yuccas and cordylines; the Rock Dell, where Canary Island aeoniums and Central American agaves thrive on the sun-baked terraces; and the Woodland Garden, a quiet, shady area where Japanese maples and flowering dogwoods, including *Cornus kousa* and *Cornus florida*, abound.

Unlike many gardens based in the West Country that have acidic moisture retentive soils, Overbeck's is predominantly alkaline and free-draining. In contrast, there are few spring-flowering rhododendrons and camellias to be seen in this garden, however there is a splendid *Magnolia campbellii*, which is over 100 years old and reliably produces masses of pink goblet-shaped flowers each March against a backdrop of the Salcombe coastline.

The Salcome Estuary from Overbeck's
(*Image courtesy of Becks, Flickr*)

❊ PAIGNTON ZOO & BOTANICAL GARDENS

Do not be put off by the name, because the grounds and gardens of Paignton Zoo are horticulturally worthy and make an excellent and extremely interesting garden visit at any time of year. Not only that, the zoo is at the forefront of animal and plant conservation and a leading light in the breeding of endangered species.

Paignton was the first zoo in the country to combine animals and a botanic garden. Originally laid out in 1923 in a hidden valley with grand old trees, secret glades, lawns, lakes and streams, this garden landscape now covers 80 acres (32 hectares) and includes five main habitat areas – wetlands, desert, savannah, temperate forest and tropical forest. Within these habitats the garden areas are themed geographically and botanically and plant selection is governed by aesthetics, plant toxicity, their suitability for association with particular animals and the need to recreate the natural habitats that individual animals would experience in the wild.

There are three glasshouses that contain tender and tropical plants from around the world. One contains a desert exhibit with cacti, succulents and other plants from arid regions. A further area is representative of a rainforest complete with birds and reptiles. ▶

Lake surrounded by *Gunnera manicata*

◀ In 2010 the 'Amphibian Ark' water gardens were created; these include seven ponds and interpretation about helping local wetland wildlife. The most recent area developed has been named 'Crocodile Swamp' and displays plants from tropical wetland areas.

Outside the glasshouses, the warm climate experienced on the south Devon coast allows the zoo to grow a wide range of tender plants from around the world. Palms, bananas and citrus are among the plants that contribute to the tropical feel found throughout much of Paignton's landscape and a garden of subtropical plants is located close to the restaurant. There is also an excellent garden of medicinal plants that surrounds the veterinary centre and the zoo currently holds the National Collection (NCCPG – Plant Heritage) of Buddleja.

One of the most significant plant-based initiatives at Paignton Zoo in recent years has been 'VertiCrop', the world's first public high-density vertical plant growing system. This working prototype shows how technology could help solve the world's food production problems. It combines high density production and the reduced need for resources such as land and water. It also enables staff to produce fresh, tasty herbs and leaf vegetables for the animals right on site, thereby eliminating the environmental impact of food miles.

◀ Echiums at Paignton Zoo   Wildflower meadow

✤ PINETUM PARK & PINELODGE GARDENS

Pinetum Park and Pine Lodge Gardens is perhaps not one of the best known gardens in Cornwall, however it is one of the finest. Situated close to St Austell, this 30-acre (12-hectare) garden is immaculately maintained and contains a fascinating collection of more than 6,000 different types of plants, many of which are labelled, something that even the most famous gardens sometimes have difficulty achieving.

Here you will find a series of gardens, all with a different focus or theme. As the name suggests, there is, of course, a pinetum, which does not simply mean a collection of pines but is in fact a fascinating collection of all different types of conifers. Throughout the gardens there are magnolias, camellias, rhododendrons and azaleas, all plants which are indicative of a Cornish garden. Complementing these are formal gardens full of rare and unusual plants, many of which originate from the Mediterranean and the Southern Hemisphere. Four-season appeal is here in abundance; there are drifts of spring bulbs, beds full of summer herbaceous plants, scores of autumn-leaf colouring shrubs and an excellent two-acre (0.8-hectare) Winter Garden, designed by Shirley Clemo, in memory of Bryan Tucker and opened in 2005. ▸

Pinetum Park   Moss and stone in the Japanese Garden ▸

◀ Water is a constant theme at Pine Lodge Gardens; there are lakes and islands where rare black swans nest and a koi carp pool surrounded by scented plants, including a delightful white wisteria which weaves its way across an arching Monet-style ornamental bridge. A bog garden hosts not only large-leaved gunneras, rheums and astilbes but also thriving populations of newts, dragonflies and herons.

Beyond the garden, tracts of open parkland dotted with mature oaks are reminiscent of an English Lancelot 'Capability' Brown landscape, and tucked away between the main garden and the parkland is a tranquil Zen Shakii garden with an authentic Japanese teahouse.

All the plants in this garden have been grown from seed kindly supplied by Kyoto Botanical Garden in Japan. This is a place to both relax and reflect, a place to allow all your senses to be awakened by the fragrances, sights, sounds and tactile plants on display. Run your hand across the cushioned tops of moisture-laden moss before allowing it to drift along the nearby granite stone seats, such a simple act that will leave your senses tingling and create a memory for life. As will a visit to Pinetum Park & Pinelodge Gardens; take my word for it, I promise you won't be disappointed.

Japanese Garden

❋ RHS ROSEMOOR

Originally a private garden of 8 acres (3.2 hectares) created by Lady Anne Berry over a thirty-year period from 1959, Rosemoor is today one of the jewels in the crown of the Royal Horticultural Society. Lady Anne gave her garden, along with a further 32 acres (13 hectares) of land, to the RHS in 1988. It was the Society's first regional garden and second only to Wisley – to which the new gardens created since Lady Anne's time bear a definite similarity.

Today the whole garden extends to 65 acres (26 hectares) and includes new formal gardens which lie just beyond the modern visitor reception building.

It is hard to comprehend that not much more than a couple of decades ago this area was grazed by sheep. Immaculate hedges of yew, beech, hornbeam, box and holly provide green walls to a series of Hidcotesque garden rooms, each with a different theme. The rose garden contains over 2,000 roses from 200 cultivars and is neighboured by potager, herb and cottage gardens, a foliage garden and a series of colour-themed gardens. Bisecting all is a 430-foot-long (150-metre) border packed with bulbs, annuals, perennials, shrubs and small trees especially chosen to provide four-season colour and interest. ▶

Colour-themed gardens

◀ Beyond the formal gardens lies a bog garden and lake. Fed by a natural stream, the lake is both ornamental and functional, acting as an irrigation reservoir for the entire garden. Fringed by gunnera, ferns, astilbes, persicaria and other large-leaved foliage plants, it offers the perfect contrast to the formal gardens and somewhere to relax before entering the fruit and vegetable garden, where the ability of the RHS to demonstrate best practice really comes to the fore. Organic gardening, green manures, crop rotation, biological controls and companion plantings are just some of the displays on offer.

No visit to Rosemoor is complete without entering Lady Anne's garden. Here the atmosphere is still that of a private garden, retaining both a sense of tranquillity and timelessness. To the northern end is Rosemoor House, built around 1780 as a fishing lodge for Lady Anne's ancestors. By the time the RHS took over, this garden already contained more than 3,500 plants collected from all over the world, including several Collingwood Ingram cherry introductions. The society have continued apace with further introductions, many of which are displayed in a delightful exotic garden, where palms and bananas sit comfortably alongside Indian ginger lilies *Hedychium sp.* and castor oil plants.

◀ Vegetable Garden

Mediterranean Garden

✤ SALTRAM HOUSE

Saltram House and its 23-acre (9-hectare) garden are positioned on a ridge with fine views over the Plym Estuary. Within the stewardship of the National Trust since 1957, the garden was originally laid out in 1743 but has received several overlays since then, principally in the Victorian era and latterly in the twentieth century.

There are three eighteenth-century buildings: the Castle Folly, an octagonal building surmounted by battlements with views towards the sea; a white Doric orangery used to house orange and lemon trees during the winter months; and a classical garden house named Fanny's Bower after the diarist Fanny Burney, who visited Saltram in 1789 along with King George III.

Linking the Castle Folly with the western aspect of the house is a fine 273-yard-long (250-metre) avenue of lime trees *Tilia x europaea*, beneath which swathes of yellow and cream-coloured narcissi display in spring and magenta-coloured flowers of *Cyclamen hederifolium* in autumn.

Near the house is the Orange Grove, designed in 1782 as a summer 'standing out' ground for citrus trees from the orangery. It performs the same function today and has at its centre a pond fringed by marsh marigolds *Caltha palustris* and flag iris *Iris pseudocorus*. Upon the surrounding gravel, white metal seats flanked by citrus in white Italianate tubs give a distinct Mediterranean feel to the grove. ▶

Castle Folly

Lime Avenue ▶

◀ If you venture into the vegetation beyond, the whole world is revealed with Australian bottlebrushes *Callistemon citrinus*, Chilean lantern trees *Crinodendron hookerianum* and Himalayan ginger lilies *Hedychium gardnerianum* all jostling for position.

Close by, the Long Border was designed in 1964 by the late Graham Stuart Thomas, the first Gardens Advisor to the National Trust. It was restored to its original design in 2009 to mark the centenary of his birth, and brings colour and interest from June until October with its inspirational selection of plants ranging from arums to acanthus and sages to sedum. Standing at the furthest end of the border are fine specimens of Chinese banana *Musa basjoo*.

By far the largest area of the garden is beyond the West Lawn and along the North Path. Here, billowing borders, once dark evergreen Victorian shrubberies, pinch the wide expanses of lawn into sinuous glades as their burgeoning collection of tender exotics rapidly expand in Saltram's mild maritime climate. Perhaps two of the finest examples on display are cinnamon-barked myrtles *Luma apiculata* and the exquisite water-lily-like blooms of *Michelia (Magnolia) doltsopa*.

The Long Border

❀ THE GARDEN HOUSE

The present Garden House dates from the early nineteenth century, however, the history of this 10-acre (4-hectare) site goes back much further and is closely entwined with nearby Buckland Abbey. In 1305 the abbey's abbot was instructed to build a house for the parish priest and this location was chosen. During the Dissolution of the Monasteries, the abbot became the vicar of Buckland Monachorum and by the early 1700s the vicarage consisted of a substantial three-storey dwelling. The remains of this original building, a tower with spiral staircase and a thatched barn, are today romantic ruins on the lower terrace of the present walled garden.

Just after the Second World War, the Garden House was purchased by Lionel Fortescue and his wife Katharine. Lionel was the son of a Newlyn school painter and had a good eye for colour as well as being an excellent plantsman. They immediately set about renovating and developing the garden while at the same time running a thriving market garden business, providing stock plants for growers in the Tamar Valley.

Assisted by their head gardener Keith Wiley, for twenty-five years, and two notable head gardeners since then, Matt Bishop and Nick Haworth, they turned the original garden and a further 6 acres (2.4 hectares) of paddocks into what is today a truly remarkable garden that takes its influence from the natural world. ▶

The Cottage Garden

❋ THE GARDEN HOUSE

◂ Covering 8 acres (3.2 hectares), this inspirational garden, or to be more accurate series of gardens, blends seamlessly into the timeless Devon landscape and offers stunning views in all directions. In total there are over 6,000 different varieties of plants here, all used to great effect in both traditional and naturalistic planting styles. A new feature created for the Golden Jubilee of the Fortescue Garden Trust, which now owns and administers the garden, is a 2-acre (0.8-hectare) arboretum with lake and ornamental bridges.

In spring there are magnificent collections of camellias, magnolias and rhododendrons to admire, as well as a bulb meadow with masses of woodland plants such as erythroniums, anemones, cyclamen and bluebells. In summer it is the walled garden built around the medieval ruins that commands attention, as well as wisteria-clad bridges, a romantic cottage garden, wild flower meadow, summer garden and quarry garden.

In autumn a glade of Japanese maples *Acer palmatum* cultivars provides a kaleidoscope of autumnal leaf tints. There is also a plant sales area with an excellent range of quality plants, including many that are grown in the garden.

◂ Wildflower mix with Trish's Bench and Summer House

Bottom terrace borders

❋ TREBAH

Trebah garden is set in a steep wooded valley that tumbles 250 feet (77 metres) from a fine Georgian house at its head to the sandy bay of Polgwidden Cove below. The view from the lawn in front of the house, over vast clumps of rhododendrons, tree ferns, bamboos and giant-leaved gunnera, to the Helford Estuary beyond, is truly spectacular.

Extending to 25 acres (10.1 hectares), Trebah was first planted over 175 years ago by Charles Fox, a member of a large Quaker family who were prosperous shipping agents and enthusiastic gardeners. Collectively they created several gardens in Cornwall including Penjerrick, Rosehill and Glendurgan, stocking them with exotic plants – many of which had not been grown in Britain before.

After a period of some decline in the middle of the twentieth century, the garden was rejuvenated by the late Tony Hibbert MBE MC and latterly the Trebah Garden Trust, and today contains a collection of more than 5,000 plants including rare subtropical species. There are 4 miles of footpaths, pools, cascades and lakes, as well as an award-winning visitor centre and restaurant.

While much overused, the statement 'a garden for all seasons', is entirely appropriate here, for such is the strength of the plant collection no matter what time of year that there will always be something in flower or looking its best. ▶

View to the Helford

Mallard Pond and Blue Bridge ▶

◀ By late February the garden is already alive with colour from sulphur-yellow flowering Australian acacias, such as the Oven's Wattle *Acacia pravissima* and Asian magnolias, including *Magnolia campbellii*, which produces rose-pink goblet-shaped blooms on a spreading canopy over 80 feet (25 metres) tall.

Camellias, rhododendrons, handkerchief trees *Davidia involucrata* and deciduous azaleas all carry flowering through to early summer, when attention switches to the sunny south-facing terraces and borders below the house and visitor centre. Here, plants from warmer regions of the world 'strut their stuff', including *Echium pininana* which sends up sky-blue flower spikes 10 feet (3 metres) tall alongside magenta and orange-coloured blooms of Canary Island compatriots *Geranium maderense* and *Isoplexis canariensis*. If the heat of the open terraces becomes too much, head for the cool tranquillity of the koi pool or the shade of the tree ferns, (some of the very first planted in Britain in 1880), where you will find delicate leaved Japanese maples *Acer palmatum*. These fill the garden with autumn leaf colour alongside hundreds of flowering hydrangeas, reflecting blue, white and pink shades in the still water of Mallard Pond through until Christmas.

Trebah tree ferns

❋ TRELISSICK

Not only is Trelissick one of the most beautiful gardens in the West Country, it also benefits from having a superb location. Even the views from the National Trust car park at its entrance are stunning – straight down the Carrick Roads, a deep navigable channel of water which stretches to Falmouth Bay.

Water is never far away at Trelissick, this 25-acre (10-hectare) garden is positioned high on a wooded peninsula with Lamouth Creek to the north, River Fal to the east and Carrick Roads and Channels Creek to the south and west. Even when immersed in the lush vegetation of the garden you may hear the chains of the King Harry Ferry as it crosses to the Roseland Peninsula. Not only that, the River Fal is deep and navigable, so it is possible to see large container ships slide past at eye level, despite the river being 100 feet (30 metres) below.

The bones of this 25-acre (10-hectare) garden were laid out during the nineteenth century and many of the larger pines and oaks date from then. However, the present abundance of ornamental plantings owes much to Ida and Ronald Copeland who inherited the estate in 1937. Over the following eighteen years, they transformed the garden, planting numerous cherries, camellias, rhododendrons and hydrangeas in the process. ▸

River Fal beyond the garden

❁ TRELISSICK

◀ The garden was given to the National Trust in 1955, but the house remains with the family.

Trelissick is not just another wild Cornish garden where rampaging 'Cornish Red' rhododendrons smother all but the most stalwart shade bearers. Here you will find manicured lawns, neatly edged beds, well maintained paths and delightful intimate spaces. This is the case for the Parsley Garden, once home to vegetables, flowers and herbs for the house but now growing choice ornamentals such as *Azara integrifolia*, *Clematis rehderiana* and *Cestrum aurantiacum*. Today, herbaceous borders surround the old kitchen garden and on the main lawn a magnificent Japanese cedar *Cryptomeria japonica* stretches its mighty branches over deep borders full of large-leaved exotics such as Japanese bananas *Musa basjoo*, cannas and ginger lilies.

Beyond the bridge that crosses the road leading to the King Harry Ferry lies Carcadden. Once an orchard, it was absorbed into the garden in the 1960s and now hosts an excellent collection of rare and unusual trees and shrubs, laid out with aesthetical aplomb in a way that few other gardens or arboreta seem able to achieve.

◀ Not just another rhododendron garden

Cherry blossom in Carcadden

❋ TRENGWAINTON

Situated just inland from Penzance, Trengwainton takes full advantage of the mild temperatures, long growing season and bountiful rain that characterises this south-western tip of the Cornish peninsular. For this is a real plantsman's garden, 25 acres (10 hectares) full of lush subtropical foliage and rare exotic plants all wrapped up in a Tolkien-like landscape of mosses, ferns and lichens.

The garden's germination began in 1814 when Rose Price, the son of a wealthy Jamaican sugar planter, purchased the estate and began to subdue the Atlantic winds with plantations of native ash, sycamore, beech and Monterey pine *Pinus radiata*. In the lee of his maturing shelterbelts, he constructed a series of walled gardens with south-sloping raised beds designed to take full advantage of the sun's warmth. So successful was this design, the beds yielded vegetables all year round. Today, some of these historically important constructions are still used for vegetable growing, as well as displaying tender exotic trees and shrubs seldom seen growing outside in the British Isles. Ribbonwood *Plagianthus regius* from New Zealand, *Lomatia ferruginea* from Argentina and Chile, *Melaleuca squarrosa* from Australia, *Magnolia doltsopa* from China, *Cestrum elegans* from Mexico and the exquisitely scented *Prostanthera lasianthos* from Tasmania all thrive within this unique microclimate. ▶

Silver Jubilee Garden

The Stream Garden ▶

◀ Even away from the walled compartments, plants of all genera and origins excel in this garden including tender rhododendrons such as fragrant flowering *Rhododendron maddenii* from Vietnam and Myanmar (Burma). A good number of Trengwainton's rhododendrons came from Frank Kingdon-Ward's 1927/28 plant-hunting expedition to north-east Assam and the Mishimi Hills in Upper Myanmar. By then the property was owned by Lt-Col Sir Edward Bolitho and it was he, along with his head gardener Alfred Creek, who designed much of the garden layout that can be seen today, including the stream garden, fringed with astilbes, candelabra primulas, arum lilies and lysichitons, which follows the broad sweeping carriage drive from garden entrance to house. Away from the drive, pathways plunge into dense vegetation before opening into a succession of themed glades, ponds and bridges. Here you will find the Silver Jubilee Garden, plantings of bamboos and grasses and sections devoted to Australasian tree ferns.

Lt-Col Sir Edward Bolitho gave the garden to the National Trust in 1961; the house is not open to the public, but the terrace and lawn in front of the house (where guinea fowl abound) reveal magnificent views over Mount's Bay to the Lizard Peninsula.

Paths dripping with rhododendrons

❧ TRESCO ABBEY GARDENS

Clustered in the Atlantic Ocean just 27 miles south-west of Land's End are 140 islands and islets collectively known as The Isles of Scilly. Here, due to the ameliorating effect of the seaborne North Atlantic Drift, the climate is mild, with an average annual temperature of 11.8 C and frost and snow are rare. Unfortunately, wind is not and these exposed rocky granite outcrops are at the mercy of regular Atlantic gales. For plants to grow successfully they have to be sheltered, either by higher ground, walls or dense plantations of trees, however, where this is achieved it is astonishing what will grow.

Nowhere is this more evident than in the 17-acre (6.9-hectare) Abbey Gardens on Tresco, where exotic plants thrive upon its sun-baked terraces and within its glades. The garden was created by Augustus Smith from 1834, the year he was appointed Lord Proprietor of Scilly and came to live on Tresco. Having built a house just above the ruins of a twelfth-century priory, he turned his attention to a garden, initially constructing a series of walled enclosures around the priory, then three long terraces interlinked by stone steps. ▶

Tresco Abbey ruins

❊ TRESCO ABBEY GARDENS

By 1855, the garden contained thriving collections of exotic plants from Africa, the Canary Islands and South America, including specimens of the Chilean bromeliad *Puya alpestris*, which produces magnificent spikes of jade-blue waxy flowers. Augustus Smith died in 1872 and five generations later it is Robert Dorrien-Smith, who, with the help of Garden Curator Mike Nelhams, manages what has been described as 'a mad mix of plants which have no right to be growing anywhere near the British Isles'. Tresco is truly unique, 255 different types of plants flower on New Year's Day alone! However, don't be fooled that this is simply a botanical collection of 20,000 exotic plants grown together because they can be. Thoughtful planting and landscaping has ensured the aesthetics of this garden are paramount. Rock walls and the remains of the priory provide structure and backdrop for foliage and flower, while clearings in the vegetation reveal stunning vistas across the sea to neighbouring islands. If ever there was a compelling reason for holidaying in the UK rather than overseas, then this is it. Where else in the world could you find Mediterranean palms, Tasmanian tree ferns, New Zealand ratas, Mexican agaves, South African proteas and Canary Island geraniums, all growing together in such a beautiful location?

Tresco Children by David Wynne

At Tresco the sea is ever present

✤ TREWITHEN

It was in 1904 that George Horace Johnstone inherited Trewithen from his father and started work on his gardening masterpiece. He first planted 100 hybrids of *Rhododendron arboretum*, two of which were named after his wife 'Alison Johnstone' and one after his gardener 'Jack Skilton'. During the First World War, 300 beech trees were felled by government order for the war effort, the bulk of them from plantations directly behind the main house (built in the 1730s). This provided the space necessary for Johnstone to mark out and plan his great glade – a long lawn flanked by four deep meandering borders. A walk around this area today has been described as 'a journey around the world in eighty minutes', and with some justification. This is truly is a plantsman's garden of the highest merit with a plant collection representative of just about every region in the temperate world, and some subtropical regions as well. Adjacent to the lawn are wave upon wave of rhododendron, deciduous azalea, camellia, corylopsis, viburnum and berberis. The colour combinations are superb, in spring they breach the lawn edges with a flood of red, yellow and white flowers. Behind are larger tree rhododendrons, enkianthis, embothrium, acer, stewartia and the smaller magnolia cultivars. ▶

Trewithen House

Fragrant deciduous azaleas abound at Trewithen ▶
(Image courtesy of Kathryn Vengel, Flickr)

◀ Finally the crowning glory, where gigantic Himalayan magnolias such as *Magnolia campbellii*, white-barked birch *Betula utilis* and southern beech *Nothofagus alpina and N. obliqua* provide shade and shelter for the displays below.

In total Trewithen covers 30 acres (12 hectares) and, as well as being a Royal Horticultural Society Recommended Garden, it is also recognised as an International Camellia Society Garden of Excellence (one of only thirty in the world). Many camellia hybrids have been developed here including 'Trewithen Pink' 'Elizabeth Johnstone' and 'Glenn's Orbit', which is a seedling of Camellia 'Donation' that first flowered at Trewithen on 20 February 1962, the day American astronaut Col John Glenn completed his first orbit of earth.

Among the other garden delights to be found here is a walled garden, which was built at the same time as the house and has climbers such as the New Zealand 'lobster's claw' *Clianthus puniceus* and centuries old wisteria growing alongside the original *Ceanothus arboreus* 'Trewithen Blue'. A shady, damp dell known as the 'Cock Pit', where moss-covered rocks and tree ferns, both *Dicksonia* and *Cyathea species* thrive, there are canopy-height viewing platforms and a replica of a Victorian *camera obscura* which projects images of the surrounding plants.

The Main Lawn in springtime

❈ TYNTESFIELD

Tyntesfield is a Grade I listed Victorian Gothic house and estate, situated south of Bristol on the site of an earlier sixteenth-century hunting lodge. In the 1860s the property was purchased and extensively remodelled by wealthy English businessmen William Gibbs, who had made his fortune collecting Peruvian guano for sale as fertiliser. The result is a glorious, opulent example of an architectural style founded on the wealth and confidence of the British Empire. The estate remained with the family until the death of Richard Gibbs, the Second Lord Wraxall, in 2001, when the property was put up for sale. In June 2002, after an extensive fundraising campaign, to which 70,000 donors contributed, Tyntesfield was eventually purchased by the National Trust with the help of a grant from the National Heritage Memorial Fund.

Although Lord Wraxall had kept the extensive walled kitchen garden in production and the wider gardens maintained to a basic level, the infrastructure, garden buildings and ornamental flower gardens had been neglected and there was a need for a major restoration. While some of this work is still ongoing, much has been done in the intervening years and the Trust has encouraged volunteers, schoolchildren, trainees and the general public to get involved with the restoration wherever possible. ▶

Tyntesfield House
(*Image courtesy of Rémy Gardette, Flickr*)

❀ TYNTESFIELD

◀ Today, a visit to the gardens of Tyntesfield is a fascinating experience. From the terrace there are extensive views across Irish yews, Portuguese laurel and other evergreens to the timeless landscape of the Yeo valley beyond. Before 1917 the terrace ended in a large domed-roof conservatory. Although long gone now, the plants that grew around it are still present, including some fine magnolias and a large Chusan palm *Trachycarpus fortunei*. On the walls and balustrades of the terrace, fragrant yellow-flowering Banksian roses *Rosa banksiae* 'Lutea' and wisteria soften the architecture, while patterned beds (ten in all), are laid out with typical Victorian colourful bedding schemes of seasonally changing bulbs and annuals surrounding ornamental hollies. In the parkland beyond the terrace there is an extensive collection of ornamental and exotic trees dating from the Victorian period and a terraced rose garden, today also planted with a selection of plants not palatable to deer, such as peonies, *Nepeta* 'Six Hills Giant' and lavender. There is also a fernery, rock garden and of course the red-brick-walled kitchen garden, which includes glasshouses stocked with peaches and vines, a productive vegetable garden and a flower garden for cutting and display in the grand house.

◀ Rose Gardens
(*Image courtesy of Crabchick, Flickr*)

Wild Flower Garden
(*Image courtesy of Crabchick, Flickr*)

❀ UNIVERSITY OF BRISTOL BOTANIC GARDEN

Following a decision in 2002 to move the Bristol University Botanic Garden from its previous location to a new site close to Durdham Down, this excellent garden officially opened to the public in March 2006 and was the first new university botanic garden to have been created in the UK for almost forty years. Set around a Victorian mansion called The Holmes, which is today used as halls of residence for students, this 4.5-acre (1.77-hectare) garden, which was designed by Land Use Consultants (who also worked on the Eden Project), has successfully managed to bring together education, contemporary design and beauty in a way that is sometimes absent in other botanic gardens.

The Garden is split into four core collections – evolution, Mediterranean climate zones, local rare native flora and useful plants for medicinal, culinary and other uses. All four subjects are tackled in an inspirational and engaging fashion. Of particular merit is the Evolutionary Walk, which winds its way through a dell while charting the most important stages in the evolution of plants on land, from green algae to flowering plants. This is fascinating stuff and graphically portrays how the thousands of plants we see around us in our gardens, streets, parks and countryside came into existence. ▶

The Holmes

Evolutionary Walk ▶

◀ Close by, a large pool provides the perfect environment for a whole host of aquatic plants including water lilies, while a wetland area displays rare and endangered plants local to the Somerset levels. A rocky outcrop mimics the kind of habitat found in the locality of the Avon Gorge and displays plants that are found there including the Bristol Onion, Spiked Speedwell and Avon Gorge whitebeam *Sorbus bristoliensis*.

Other parts of the garden are zoned on a geographical and climatic basis and include collections of plants from Australasia, South Africa, Chile, California and the Mediterranean. There is also a European herb garden and a Chinese medicinal herb garden. Signage throughout the garden is excellent and the use of handwritten plant names on bright green labels seems to make the science all the more accessible.

A large glasshouse displays many exotic cacti and succulents, tropical ferns, orchids, giant Amazonian water lilies *Victoria amazonica* and the beautiful sacred lotus flower *Nelumbo nucifera*.

In total there are 4,500 plant species in this garden originating from all over the world, so there really is something for everyone, including some very fine herbaceous borders directly outside The Holmes.

The Glasshouse